Our Hopes, Our Future

Andreas M. Krafft

Our Hopes, Our Future

Insights from the Hope Barometer

 Springer

Andreas M. Krafft
St. Gallen, St. Gallen, Switzerland

ISBN 978-3-662-66204-5   ISBN 978-3-662-66205-2   (eBook)
https://doi.org/10.1007/978-3-662-66205-2

This Springer imprint is published by the registered company Springer-Verlag GmbH, DE, part of Springer Nature.
The registered company address is: Heidelberger Platz 3, 14197 Berlin, Germany

Preface

Since 2009, we have been investigating the wishes and hopes of the population in various countries of the world with the annual Hope Barometer survey. Starting from Switzerland, the survey is being carried out in cooperation with universities in Australia, France, India, Israel, Italy, Colombia, Malta, Nigeria, Austria, Poland, Portugal, Czech Republic, Spain and South Africa. The approximately 10,000 people from different age and professional groups who participate annually have provided valuable basic data in recent years to gain a deeper insight into what and how people hope in everyday life and enrich their lives. The focus is not on fear and worry, but on the desire and hope for a good and fulfilling future. Many results have already been presented and published in several scientific forums.

When we asked people in November 2019 about their expectations regarding long-term trends and future scenarios, we did not suspect that the mostly gloomy predictions would become partly painful reality in just a few months. The world has not been the same since the beginning of 2020 due to the Corona pandemic. The results from the November 2020 survey, which reports how people coped with the ensuing stressful situations and mastered them successfully, were all the more exciting. While in the first ten years of the Hope Barometer our research results provided basic insights for a better understanding of the phenomenon of hope, the years 2020 and 2021 revealed the urgency and relevance of hope in times of crisis full of uncertainty and profound changes. In many public interviews and lectures, we were able to share the knowledge of our ten-year work with people and, thanks to this, convey courage and a hopeful view of the future. The positive feedback from all over the world has shown how great the yearning for the constructive power of hope is.

The universal and existential value of hope can be best explored when we make use of various scientific disciplines. In this book, the empirical results of the Hope Barometer are integrated with the individual psychological approaches of Positive Psychology, the social science focus of future research, and the humanities findings of pragmatic philosophy. The key message of the book is not "in the end, everything will be fine", but "no matter what the future brings, we can always improve". Hope is not just putting on rose-colored glasses. Hope means that we can and should wish for a better future for each of us, for our families and for the world as a whole, and that despite or precisely in times of crisis and catastrophe, we can engage with others and do a lot of good together so that our lives will be more beautiful and worth living.

I would like to thank all the long-standing members of the international research network of the Hope Barometer for their wonderful and meaningful cooperation and for the empirical data that serve as the basis for this book: Prof. Dr. Alena Slezackova in the Czech Republic, Prof. Dr. Tharina Guse in South Africa, Prof. Dr. Charles Martin-Krumm and Prof. Dr. Fabien Fenouillet in France, Prof. Dr. Elżbieta Kasprzak and Dr. Patryk Stecz in Poland, Dr. Dorit Redlich-Amirav in Israel, Prof. Dr. Carmel Cefai in Malta, Prof. Dr. Maria Valle Flores-Lucas in Spain, Prof. Dr. Helena Águeda Marujo in Portugal, Bertram Strolz in Austria, Prof. Dr. Rajneesh Choubisa and Dr. Chitra Nair in India, Dr. Mark Sinclair in Australia, Prof. Dr. Stella Conte in Italy, Prof. Dr. Eduardo Wills Herrera in Colombia and Dr. JohnBosco Chika Chukwuorji in Nigeria.

Andreas M. Krafft

Contents

1

Introduction

The results of the Hope Barometer for the years 2019 and 2020 sketch a rather dark future full of crises and show the psychological consequences of such scenarios. If we as individuals and as a society are to flourish, we need images of a hopeful world that will promote our commitment and cohesion. But what does it take to ignite the flame of hope for a livable future together without a naive optimism trivializing and playing down the current problems? Hope contains the belief in a better world but also the recognition of obstacles and the motivation to act. This book presents the phenomenon of hope in connection with individual psychological findings and socially relevant developments. After the psychological basics of future thinking, the general expectations and wishes for the future of around 10,000 people from fourteen countries are presented. The experiences of the Corona pandemic give hope because they show how people can deal successfully with crises. This results in the importance and character of individual and social hope.

1.1 Looking into the Future

Almost every day the media report on some crisis or catastrophe. In addition to the worldwide Corona pandemic, which determined most areas of our lives in 2020 and 2021, reports of natural disasters, ecological disasters and social and human tragedies are increasing. But in times of crisis, new forms of hope and confidence also arise. People show solidarity with the victims, artists encourage the population, and communities engage in new relief and development initiatives.

Since 2009, we have been investigating the future expectations and hopes of the population with the annual Hope Barometer. In the years 2019 and 2020, around 10,000 people from fourteen countries on various continents

© The Author(s), under exclusive license to Springer-Verlag GmbH, DE, part of Springer Nature 2022
A. M. Krafft, *Our Hopes, Our Future*, https://doi.org/10.1007/978-3-662-66205-2_1

took part in this study. A key result of the barometer is the finding that, on the one hand, the majority of people look hopefully into the future for their private lives, but on the other hand, they are mostly pessimistic about social development (Krafft & Walker, 2018).

Most future studies show that the expectations of the population, i.e. what most people consider likely in the future, differ almost diametrically from their ideals and hopes. The coming decades will be seen as an age of crises and problems rather than one of peace and prosperity, especially in the rich countries of Europe. It looks quite different when young people in particular sketch their visions and hopes for desired future images. In the dreams of most young people, the individual, competition and material well-being are less emphasized than community, family, cohesion and environment.

Most people recognize to a large extent what is not going well in the world, be it in the economy, in global politics or in social and ecological areas. Unlike in previous epochs, however, there is currently no common vision of a desired future. Against the background of manifold economic, technological, social and ecological trends, many people complain of a lack of positive future images that could convey hope and enthusiasm.

These findings can be related to the thesis of the German philosopher Jürgen Habermas (1985), who already diagnosed an "exhaustion of utopian energies", i.e. the end of great social visions, in the 1980s. Milan Simecka (1984, p. 175) once said: "A world without utopias would be a world without social hope – a world of resignation to the status quo". This would be a world without ideals and without positive future designs. According to Viktor Frankl (1979), cynicism, conformism and totalitarianism (e.g. in the form of nationalism), phenomena that can already be observed in some places today, are the greatest enemies of hope (Halpin, 2002).

How people look to the future, whether with hope, fear or indifference, will influence the way they think and act in the here and now. We cannot change the past, but we have a shared interest in creating a livable and sustainable future. There is therefore a need, especially in today's time, to develop positive images of the future so that especially young people can think about the world in which they would like to live in the future. If they do not let themselves be infected by the negative reports in the media and the bad mood in their environment, people are quite capable of imagining a better future. This requires not only cognitive abilities, but also people's feelings, values, attitudes, wishes, hopes and dreams.

1.2   The Value of Hope

Barbara Fredrickson (2013) has placed the function and significance of positive emotions in an evolutionary context. Just as negative emotions like fear and worry were necessary for human survival, positive emotions like hope, confidence and joy are the foundation for the actual development and progress of humanity. While fear and worry narrow our perception, positive emotions expand our thinking to new possibilities.

A positive attitude can help us manage difficult situations in life better. Hope and confidence strengthen us in good times and make us more resilient in bad times. Hope can foster development of a certain calmness in difficult moments. We can distance ourselves from the problems, see the bigger picture, and possibly also find something good in a difficult situation. Hope expands our ways of thinking and observation, and builds positive resources for managing negative situations.

Hope gives the view of everyday life new perspectives and new horizons. Because we also look at the good side of things and do not remain negative, new impressions and possibilities arise in our consciousness. Thus, thanks to a positive view of the future, people become more creative. New ideas arise, and the attitude towards life itself changes. Previously burdensome problems evolve into challenges, the future opens up new options, and previously unknown solutions come into being.

At the same time, hope promotes personal growth. Positive emotions build us up and expand our perception and consciousness. Self-confidence is strengthened, and we develop an open attitude towards new events and other people. The expansion of consciousness causes us to think not only of ourselves but also of others and to feel connected with a greater whole. When we feel confident, we are friendlier and more helpful, want to do good, and work more intensively with other people.

1.3   Shaping the Future Together

If we let ourselves be guided by the ideas of great philosophers like Immanuel Kant, Ernst Bloch and John Dewey, individual goals can be linked to visions of a good life in a better world, whereby a new and more fundamental hope for happiness and fulfillment can awaken in people. Such a desirable future can at least partially occur if we can imagine it mentally today and shape it step by step together. The hope for a better future can best be defined as a greater social process of hope and planning.

Transforming the world goes hand in hand with changing oneself and every individual, whereby the central importance of human values and virtues is automatically addressed (Hicks, 2003). The goal of this hope is the connection of individual and social "flourishing", which can be translated as "flourishing" in German and denotes the process of personal and social growth. It is about the development and unfolding of one's own abilities and potentials in connection with the design of a sustainable and characteristically integral way of life with which the whole world can flourish again. Hope is the opposite of fear and worry as well as of apathy and discouragement because it inspires the belief and trust in the achievability of a flourishing future.

This pragmatic hope consists of a series of habits thanks to which we create new possibilities of working together with others and thus making the world a better place. Such hope gives us the motivation, as West (2009, 217) says, "to continue to fight for more love, more justice, more freedom and more democracy". In order to promote one's own as well as the collective well-being, we must take a long-term, global perspective and use our personal strengths and abilities to shape a socially and ecologically sustainable society. This does not always mean that everyone has to trigger a great social revolution. Most of the time it is enough if people make a difference in their immediate environment through their empathetic, caring and helpful behavior.

1.4   Structure of the Book

In this book we offer an approach that starts from the possibilities and abilities of the individual and at the same time takes a global perspective as the field of action. Changes and transformations usually do not happen overnight and require the shoulder-to-shoulder of personal and social resources in a medium- to long-term time dimension. The integration of future-oriented social science, positive psychology and pragmatic philosophy combines individual and social flourishing with a view to the hopes of a desirable world in the context of current and future societal trends and scenarios.

The book is divided into three parts: the psychology of future thinking, coping with crises and shaping the future. Part One begins with an introduction to how people think about the future. The psychology of future thinking has dealt intensively with this question at the individual level. This is followed by a discussion of the design of various future images out of the conviction that we should not only adapt to the future, but that we can actively and responsibly shape it. Based on the research, we illuminate here the diverse modes of thinking about the future and the importance of expectations, trends, and possible as well as desirable future scenarios. Positive future images are closely linked to people's hopes and are generally an important source of hope.

In this context we refer to humanistic future research, which deals less with technological developments than with people's fears, concerns and hopes as well as their behavior as a social science discipline. In addition, it contributes to positive development by helping to design future images that stimulate value concepts, motivation, critical and creative thinking, imagination, a willingness to change and a sense of responsibility.

This first part of the book presents the international results of the Hope Barometer from November 2019, i.e. a few months before the outbreak of the Corona pandemic. Around 10,000 people in fourteen countries were asked about their expectations, hopes and fears for the future in various areas of society, about long-term trends, about the development of the quality of life, about likely and desirable scenarios, and about their assumptions regarding the world.

Part Two of the book deals with the experiences of another 10,000 people during the pandemic year 2020. The Hope Barometer from November 2020 examines the various coping strategies of people in dealing with experienced stress situations, the central role of hope in successfully overcoming the crisis, and the psychological consequences in the form of stress-related growth. It may seem strange that we are not—like so many other studies—concerned with the negative consequences of the crisis, but rather focus on hope, personal and social resources, and positive effects. The years 2020 and 2021 have put almost everyone to a tough test. The key question is how people in general and society as a whole can deal positively with this crisis on the assumption that we can make a bad situation worse or we can improve the situation, learn from it, change and grow through a constructive attitude and our behavior.

With further results of the Hope Barometer and on the basis of philosophical and psychological findings, Part Three is dedicated to the question of how we together can shape a better future against the backdrop of current and future crises. The essential theoretical foundations for this are the writings of classic philosophers such as Ernst Bloch and Gabriel Marcel, of many contemporary philosophers and psychologists, and of authors such as Victoria McGeer, Richard Rorty and Patrick Shade, who, inspired by forerunners of pragmatic philosophy, above all John Dewey, have carefully examined the phenomenon of hope and shown its worth for a successful life and a better world. On this basis, we develop a model of hope and present the individual elements and concrete practices for a hopeful life.

As part of a master's lecture on the psychology of hope, students at the University of St. Gallen carried out two exercises in designing positive future images, the essential focus of which is presented in Part Three in anonymous and summarized form in order to explain the conceptual basis. On the one hand, the 28 students aged 22 to 41 designed a portrait of their "Best Possible Self" based on their personal preferences and interests. On the other hand, they designed and described individual images of the best possible future world from their point of view. The two exercises are effective interventions for a positive attitude to life and a valuable basis for personal commitment. It is possible to imagine concretely what makes life worth living and what paths can lead to a good life. These images reveal the ideals, values and dreams of young adults. In addition, the essential experiences and reflections on the effect of the two future exercises are evaluated, and valuable insights and conclusions are drawn from them.

The book ends with practical hints for developing positive habits for designing a hopeful life in community with others. The practical value of hope is not only connected to a distant future, but manifests itself in everyday life as we live here and now. Positive habits of hope are based on virtues and strengths such as creativity, openness to new things, commitment, perseverance, patience, humility, trust, determination, willpower, courage, solidarity, helpfulness and a belief in good. If these strengths become habits, they form the basis for a hopeful character and a hopeful society. Crises are also a good opportunity for us to cultivate and further develop these habits.

Part I

Images of the Future

2

Psychology of Future Thinking

People who think about the future shape their lives more consciously, sustainably and responsibly. This is not about predicting future events, but about looking ahead to a desirable future that one can commit oneself to in the present. The future is an arena of diverse possibilities and not a linear succession of predetermined events. In order for people to shape the future positively, they must first imagine it creatively, but then also set specific goals and overcome possible difficulties. Unrealistic optimism can create a positive mood, but it can also lead to an overestimation of one's abilities and an underestimation of the challenges that arise. A look into the future takes on a special meaning when we can meaningfully connect our past and present with our future images. Good and bad experiences shape the way we see and shape the future. Emotions and socially accepted ideas play an important role.

2.1 Why We (Should) Think About the Future

How people think about the future and prepare for possible desired and undesired future events is known in psychology as future-oriented thinking (Aspinwall, 2005; Baumeister et al., 2018; Oettingen, 1997; Seligman et al., 2016). A special ability of us human beings is that we can imagine various future events, outcomes and states, and based on these ideas we can orient our behavior. Our thoughts about what the future will look like have a significant influence on our current decisions and activities. Before we decide to do something, we can assess the immediate as well as the far-reaching consequences of our actions. We can also weigh between long-term and short-term interests and forego immediate pleasure if we can gain valuable results in the future. For example, every student or pupil has already

© The Author(s), under exclusive license to Springer-Verlag GmbH, DE, part of Springer
Nature 2022
A. M. Krafft, *Our Hopes, Our Future*, https://doi.org/10.1007/978-3-662-66205-2_2

experienced that it is sometimes better to forego a social get-together with friends in order to be able to prepare better for an exam. Only because we think in a future-oriented way can we engage in important areas of life. For example, one will only embark on an apprenticeship or a university degree if one promises oneself a fulfilling and well-paid job in the future.

The way we think about the future depends on our past and our social environment. Our view of the future is influenced by previous experiences, current conditions and our own attitude towards ourselves and our environment (Krafft, 2019). Bad experiences make us more cautious or pessimistic, and the degree of self-confidence and trust in others strengthens our resolve and stamina. Our way of thinking about the future is balanced when we take both the positive and the negative aspects into account so that we can achieve the positive things in life and avoid the negative ones.

People who are future-oriented usually take on more responsibility for decisions they make today, the consequences of which will only be seen in a few years. For example, loans are taken out more carefully or health-damaging behavior such as incorrect nutrition or smoking is avoided. If we think about the future and act proactively such as by carrying out preventive health checks, we can deal with smaller difficulties early on before they develop into bigger problems.

Thinking about the future is important for solving problems and achieving personal goals as well as for developing and implementing new ideas. It is even assumed nowadays that daydreaming and fantasizing have a highly positive impact on our behavior and further development.

2.2 Retrospection, Prediction and Prospection

For decades psychology has emphasized that our behavior is determined by the past. The latest research on future thinking suggests that we are less "pushed" by the past than "pulled" by the future (Seligman et al., 2013). The realization that human consciousness and behavior are more oriented towards the future than towards the past has the potential, from the perspective of psychology, to offer profound new insights that may result in a new understanding of human nature (Baumeister et al., 2016).

People differ from other living things in that they are able to think consciously about future events. The term "prospection" is used as the opposite of "retrospection" and refers to thinking about the future (Gilbert & Wilson, 2007). Recent studies show that in everyday life we humans have more thoughts about the future than about the past (Baumeister et al.,

2016). The reason for this is that while the past can no longer be changed, the future can be shaped in many different ways. Thinking about the future is pragmatic in that it can influence and improve future situations. The brain uses information from the past to create thoughts about the present and the future. Even the term "better" suggests that there are different, more or less good alternatives available.

The theory of pragmatic prospection (Baumeister et al., 2016) states that people think about the future in order to direct their actions towards desired results. Pragmatic prospection takes place when we think about the future in a way that has a practical use, in the sense of a process for generating desired future outcomes and avoiding undesired consequences.

The difference between pragmatic prospection and mere prediction is particularly relevant here. A prediction is a mental representation of a future event or behavior, an assessment of whether this event or behavior is likely to occur or not. A prediction is about an assumption of what will happen. It focuses on a specific result. Common ideas of fate, destiny, predestination and determinism say that a certain future is already inevitable and could in principle be known from the present. The common idea that the future is to some extent already inevitable and should be foreseen as best as possible does not fit well with how we actually imagine the future in the form of eventualities, options and new possibilities.

According to the latest psychological findings, prediction is not the main function of foresight. Current studies show that when people think about the future, they imagine it as a portfolio of various possibilities rather than as the unfolding of predetermined events. Baumeister and his colleagues have called such future thinking a "matrix of maybe" (Baumeister & Tice, 1985; Baumeister et al., 2018). We humans see the future as a series of options rather than as a linear development. The goal is less a prediction of what will happen for sure than preparation for actions in situations that are defined by a series of alternative options. There are relatively few certainties and many unknowns, possibilities and risks. That is precisely why we see the future as uncertain and risky, but also as highly configurable and changeable. If the future could simply be predicted, there would be no room for designing it.

The main reason why we think about the future is to steer actions towards desired results (hence the pragmatic designation). The brain can imagine various futures and make meaningful decisions and control action on the basis of these mental images. With pragmatic prospection we want to assess what we can do now to shape the future. Thus, the purpose of prospection is not primarily to know what will happen, but rather to influence and, if possible, to determine what will happen. When thinking about the future, it is not a question of "What will happen?", but rather of "What do I want to happen?" Not the prediction of future reality, but the imagination of future possibilities is the primary purpose of prospection.

With our forward-thinking, we want to imagine what decisions and requirements we will be confronted with regarding multiple options. Pragmatic prospection is about various possibilities, eventualities and decisions that one has to make and with which one focuses on a variety of possible results. Only later do people think about possible obstacles and how they can overcome them to achieve their goals.

Our consciousness simulates various future scenarios that can deviate more or less from the current reality and are associated with more or less meaningful and desirable possibilities. Thus, the future is seen as a matrix of alternative possibilities. This conscious thinking about various future options activates our willpower and our ability to act. By thinking about the future as a matrix of possibilities, we can prepare for diverse situations and align our decisions with desired results.

The more conscious the thinking about the future is, the greater the variety of possible situations in our lives and their associated action options will be taken into consideration. Consciousness not only recognizes alternative possibilities, but also creates them. Thanks to our imagination, we create new future images that can differ significantly from current reality. We can therefore imagine a life and a society that differ from our current life and society. Thus, foresight is a creative and meaningful act with which one can develop several future images that contradict the current conditions and go beyond simple expectations. The more diverse the matrix of future possibilities, the greater our degree of freedom and choice. With our willpower we can influence future events, which triggers a fundamental trust in the malleability of the future.

Our conscious thinking simulates alternative possibilities and scenarios. This simulation includes further considerations such as the idea of alternative course of action options as well as necessary coping strategies if something does not go as we have wished. People think about the future in order to orient their actions. Consciousness can simulate what does not yet exist, namely that which could happen, but also that which should not happen. People who base their actions on such simulations of future possibilities and thus use this power of human consciousness are, according to the findings of Baumeister and his colleagues (Baumeister et al., 2018), much more successful in life than those who do not.

2.3 Fantasy and Reality

Through prospection a connection is established between images of the future and one's actions in the present. The ultimate goal of prospection is to align our behavior in the present on the basis of what will bring about desired future results. The mental contrasting model of Gabriele Oettingen (2000, 2012, 2014) shows how people compare their images of a desired future to current reality. Future thinking typically begins with the mental image of a desired outcome. In a first step, therefore, we formulate a wish and imagine the best possible result on the basis of it. Such wish images are usually optimistic and positive by nature. In a second phase, one thinks about how to get from the present to this desired future, and this requires the imagination of possible requirements and implementing steps. In this phase, concrete goals are formulated and possible obstacles that could stand in the way of the desired result are considered. In this thought process we determine whether achieving the result is not only desirable, but also if it is feasible. These steps can be experienced much less positively because they are based on a realistic awareness of the difficulties that need to be overcome on the way to fulfilling the wish. This stage is therefore cautious and sometimes rather pessimistic.

Purely fantasizing about an idealized future, without taking into account any obstacles, can be referred to as mere wishful thinking. Oettingen and colleagues have found that the success rates are quite low when people simply have the fantasy of an ideal future state and disregard possible obstacles and difficulties (e.g. Kappes & Oettingen, 2011; Oettingen, 2012). Therefore, mere fantasies about a positive future can be counterproductive because they reduce the energy and motivation needed to achieve the desired state. People often overestimate their abilities and do not think through the effort and the steps necessary in order to achieve the goal. In the second phase of future thinking, it is therefore essential to recognize what can go wrong on the way to achieving the goal. The person begins with the idea of an optimal result, then identifies and thinks through potential obstacles and difficulties, and finally plans how to deal with them so that the chances of success are maximized. In this way, one can better prepare for the obstacles and devise coping strategies. However, if the obstacles are very large, the person may decide that the future result is too cumbersome or simply cannot be realized regardless of how desirable it is.

While mere indulgence in positive fantasies and daydreams is rather counterproductive, fantasies when supplemented with a realistic view of the obstacles stimulate positive behavior. After all, thinking about what could go wrong is only meaningful in connection with an idea of what could go right. It is therefore necessary that we first establish a wish, then formulate the desired result, and finally also recognize the obstacles. All steps are necessary and must be carried out in exactly this order: first the idea of the future wish, then the formulation of a goal, and finally the recognition of obstacles (Oettingen et al., 2001). When people imagine the hurdles they might face before they define the wish and the goal, they focus their thoughts on the possible obstacles and problems and thereby block themselves.

2.4   Unrealistic Optimism

We human beings often experience "progress bias", i.e. we overestimate the effects of actions that bring us closer to our goal, and underestimate the possible events that can prevent us from doing so. This "progress bias" has certain advantages and disadvantages. It is usually good if we are confident because the expectation of an impending success can strongly motivate us. But success distortion can also backfire if we make less effort than necessary because we overestimate our chances of success and, on the other hand, underestimate how difficult it is and how much still needs to be done to achieve it. A less confident attitude can increase the willpower and motivation with which we can take practical steps and overcome possible difficulties (Baumeister et al., 2016).

But how does this distorted view of things come about? Our perception is psychologically shaped by what is known as the optimism bias or unrealistic optimism (Weinstein, 1980, 1989). Optimism bias is experienced, as Weinstein describes it, as a positive image of reality. In general people tend to overestimate their own future more positively than the future of other people. On the one hand, most people believe, for example, that they will be more successful and live longer than others. On the other hand, they believe that the probability of their experiencing bad things is lower than the average for the population. This optimistic assessment of the future therefore refers both to positive aspects in life such as one's own house, a good job, a high income, an expensive trip or a good marriage, and to the avoidance of negative aspects such as divorce, health problems, unemployment, becoming a victim of violence, etc. Basically, optimism bias consists of an unfounded belief that, compared to other people, specific events will turn out more favorably for oneself than can be expected on average (Shepperd et al., 2015).

In general, optimism includes the prediction of a positive, desired future, and that can be an important first step in deciding what one wants. But optimistic predictions can also be the result of superficial assessments and unconscious biases. Once you start thinking more deeply about the future, possible risks and problems come to mind, so that future images become more complex and differentiated. After imagining what you would like, you need to think about problems and obstacles, prepare for them and act accordingly. The goal of thinking about the future is to take actions and make decisions that will lead to the desired results. This requires a balance between the idea of what one wants, the conscious consideration of what could prevent it and thoughts of how that could be overcome.

2.5 Meaning and Sense

Anticipating the future includes thoughts with which a possible future is connected with present action. The value of pragmatic prospection lies in meaningful stories that relate the future and the present to each other. Current decisions should improve future results. The human ability by virtue of which we can logically connect the present with the future gives the present a sense, for example, when we work towards future goals and ideals. What is decisive is that thoughts of the future give the present a sense inasmuch as current actions are seen as part of a meaningful sequence of events leading to the desired future result. The connection between the present and the future, through which the future (and less the past) influences the present, consists of meaning. Plans are an example of the use of meaningful relationships that make it possible for the present to be guided by the future.

Baumeister et al. (2013) found that the assessment of the meaningfulness of life is related to how much people can mentally link past, present and future together (in contrast to happiness, which is positively associated with thinking about the present and the past). Human life is experienced in a meaningful narrative form in which one's current actions are part of a story that extends into the future. People construct narratives to give their lives meaning. Some of these narratives are short, others are more extensive and extend to understanding a whole life as a (somewhat) coherent narrative possibly embedded in even larger temporal contexts such as religious and political beliefs.

These meaningful narratives or thought sequences are primarily of a sociocultural and emotional nature (Baumeister & Masicampo, 2010). What makes sense and is important in life is closely related to the values and norms of our respective societies. What we desire and what we do to achieve it depends on the personal and social expectations of the right life. Furthermore, the assessment of future events and options is very much influenced by emotions. The desirability of a future result is automatically evaluated by our feelings. For example, we have the feeling that it could make us happy if a certain event were to occur in the future. Emotions play a valuable, even vital role in the evaluation of future options and the possible obstacles and difficulties that may arise. For example, a defensive pessimism can be very useful if it allows us to prepare for possible problems.

3

Forms of Thinking and Images of the Future

As long as we only want to predict the future, we miss the diverse possibilities for actively and constructively shaping it. In our perception there is not only one future, but a variety of conceivable futures. Some of these futures frighten us, others give us hope. The future arises as a result of concrete decisions and actions. The question is what should we focus on in shaping the future. For improvement of life general, technological development is assessed in the light of human needs and values. Therefore, the individual, social and ecological areas of life are of primary interest. The future is a common good that we have to create together. It is not just a continuation of the past and the present, but includes things that have not existed before. Through commitment to the future, we learn and together dedicate ourselves to something new.

3.1 Two Ways of Thinking About the Future

What we do every day and how we shape our lives depends to a large extent on the ideas we have of the future, the goals we set ourselves and the means we use to achieve them. In times of increasing complexity, confusion and uncertainty, we want to know more about what the future will look like. In most considerations and discussions about the future, we focus on the questions of what will happen in the future and how the world will look in the future. Most companies and the public tend to ask and seek the answers to these questions from the one-sided perspective of economic and technological development. A widely held view is that there should be some sort of economic and technological "weather forecast" (Kreibich, 2008), as if one could make clear predictions and thus generate "knowledge" about the future. We want to know how we will move around in the future, how we

© The Author(s), under exclusive license to Springer-Verlag GmbH, DE, part of Springer Nature 2022
A. M. Krafft, *Our Hopes, Our Future*, https://doi.org/10.1007/978-3-662-66205-2_3

will live, work and communicate with each other, what new technologies there will be and what our healthcare system will look like. The motivation behind this is the prediction of developments in a future that is still uncertain for us, about which we may already be pondering and for which we can then prepare optimally. Its foremost goal is to evoke a feeling of security and controllability.

Even though we can make certain predictions about future states based on past and current trends and experiences such as demographic development and digitalization, a clear prediction of the future is still not possible. This is because from today's perspective future events are still too unpredictable. For example, could anyone have predicted in 1970 how the world would look in 2000, 2010, or even 2020? Although many experts have known the potential risk of a pandemic for years, COVID-19 and its effects have still surprised us completely. The complexity, networking, and dynamics of our modern world make a "calculation" of the future impossible. Not only can we not clearly predict the future, but even the desire to predict the future involves a decisive danger: by focusing exclusively on a single possible future, our thought process is unnecessarily limited. Possible options available to us are then consciously or unconsciously ignored (Graf, 2003).

By trying to create security and predictability, this widespread way of thinking limits alternative future designs. However, we can change our perspective and approach by making use of uncertainty, unpredictability and unforeseeability and encouraging people to imagine alternative futures. We talk about futures in the plural because there is not just one future, but a multitude of possible visions of the future. The fundamental difference between these two ways of thinking lies in what we understand by "future": the future is not something that just happens to us, but is like an open horizon full of possibilities that can be "explored" creatively and above all in various directions. We have the power to imagine diverse futures, and we create our futures through our actions.

From a scientific point of view, this corresponds to the approach of future research in the humanities and social sciences, whereby research is understood not as knowledge of the future, but as the acquisition of knowledge of how people think about the future and how this thinking affects their decisions and actions. For every area of life, we have a wide range of possible futures available to us. The actual result is determined by our choice and behavior.

The common case of dealing with the future in the singular as if there were only one future has, from a humanistic perspective, far-reaching cultural and political implications. The idea of the "one predictable future" is seen as conformist prediction and planning of technological and economic developments. The probable future is then considered predetermined and fateful. A plural future opens up the possibility of imagining and creating alternatives to the status quo. This takes into account the complexity and networking of people in a socio-cultural context and the existing uncertainty that arises from change. There is no single, controllable future, but many possible futures that we can map, design and create together according to our wishes and ideas.

3.2   Two Contrasting Images of the Future

If one looks at the various research work and publications on the future, two contrasting world views with regard to human development can be distinguished following Markley and Harman (1982). Gidley (2017) calls these the "evolutionary-transformative", "human-centered" or "humanistic" vs. the "technological-extrapolative" or "technotopic" future image. The human-centered future image sees the future from the perspective of man and the environment. This way of looking at things starts from the economic, social and ecological consequences of the modern lifestyle. It is about solving social imbalances, political and military conflicts as well as serious environmental problems. The center of this so-called humanistic view of the future is the development of human and environmentally friendly future designs which have often been outlined in key social utopias and visions. In contrast to this are the "technotopic futures", which are dominated by robotics, genetic engineering and artificial intelligence, and which to many people can seem to be mechanistic, reductionist and ultimately dehumanizing.

However, we should not regard all future designs based on technological development as "technotopic" and hostile to man. Even if modern technologies have brought much evil, they have improved life in many ways and in countless cases have even saved it. Let's just think 100 years back and compare today's standard of living to what it was then, and not just in the rich countries of the North. Thanks to technology, many more people can be supplied with food and medical care, have a dignified home, enjoy an education and much more. In addition, the development of new technologies can offer unexpected opportunities and perspectives for solving the challenges facing humanity today.

The humanistic, social and humanities perspective has the definite advantage of being oriented towards people's needs and values and rejects a one-sided technoscientific and materialistic understanding of progress. Its central concern is with the question of how to design a sustainable and humane society and make the world a better place. The future of social science is therefore about human values and hopes as well as about visions of a better world (Masini, 2000).

This perspective is based on a positive image of human nature which includes empathy, generosity, fairness and forgiveness, as well as a commitment to live in peace and to reject violence and destruction. People are seen as agents of change, with the responsibility of maintaining the ecological balance between people, society and the earth. People-centered futures require continuous psychological, sociocultural, aesthetic and even technological development, as well as a commitment to improve concrete conditions for the entire human race through education, cultural diversity, greater economic and resource-related equality, and respect for future generations (Gidley, 2017).

3.3   Principles of Future Thinking

To deal with the future from a social science perspective, the following principles must be observed (Riner, 1987; Slaughter, 1993; Ziegler, 1991):

1. The future does not exist as an objective entity in the outside world. The future is always the result of human imagination.
2. The future does not belong to the domain of what one can know, but to the domain of what one does, i.e. of practical experience. It deals with the conscious and reflective development of specific and action-relevant images.
3. People are active, purposeful and goal-oriented beings. The future is not a phenomenon that happens to people, but rather is actively (more or less intentionally) shaped by them.
4. A society consists of patterns of social interaction. It arises and develops as an emergent result of human activity.
5. Patterns of behavior and action are determined by experiences from the past, by current decisions, and by expectations, hopes and fears in relation to the future.
6. The world and everything in it (including nature) form a larger unit. Everything is interconnected and interdependent in a natural and temporal chain of connections.

7. Not everything that will exist in the future existed in the past or already exists in the present. The future includes things that have not existed previously.
8. Thus, the future is not completely predetermined, but "open". This expands the horizon for new thoughts and design options.
9. Thinking about the future should always trigger a learning process in the sense that current conditions and developments are not understood as self-evident and inevitable.
10. One learns the most about the future in a group of learners who listen to each other and take different positions and, if possible, develop ideas of a desirable state.
11. Confrontation with the future should motivate change and action through thinking anew about traditional habits and triggering new ones.
12. Future thinking is particularly relevant when it influences action in the here and now. Future situations are influenced by current decisions and the concrete choice between various options.

Although the future cannot be studied and no certain knowledge about it exists, it is still important to deal with it, as Cornish (2001, p. 32) aptly says:

> "The paradox of the future: The future does not exist and never has existed, yet it is our most precious possession because it is all we have left. The future is where we will spend the rest of our lives."

Future research is concerned from this perspective with how people imagine the future, how their thoughts about the future influence their decisions in the present, and what they can do to realize their future visions (Hicks, 2003). It is oriented towards the human subject and its needs, and connects them with social and ecological worlds, whereby its fundamental focus becomes the general quality of life.

3.4 Three Categories of Future Thinking

People's diverse future images play an important role in the design of future life plans. Different people have different ideas about the future that need to be explored. Since it is impossible to predict the future as a single event, there can only be alternative futures. Because the future is not fully determinable, various future developments will always be possible and designable.

From today's perspective the future is fundamentally diverse and open; as Graf (2003) puts it, it is an arena of possibilities and a variety of alternatives.

For this reason, basically we need to deal with three different categories of future, namely probable, possible and desired future images and design options (Bell, 1997; Dator, 1996). Through a systematic analysis of current and expected trends, through a visionary examination of the possible, and through moral assessment of desirable possibilities, we can develop a number of alternative future images (Bell, 2009).

Probable and expected futures

So-called probable future developments do not refer only to a calculation of mathematical probability by means of which one could predict the future. Rather, it is a question of assessing what people (including experts) think is most likely to happen if current trends are taken into account. The usual question is: "What can be expected in the future if things continue as they are now?" Some developments, such as demographic structure and its consequences, can be calculated mathematically. Even if the answers to these questions are based on certain facts, the future scenarios will still be of a subjective nature (even among experts). While some people look optimistically into the future, others tend to be more pessimistic about the developments of tomorrow.

Possible and alternative futures

When considering possible or alternative futures, one looks at the world as it could become. There are two different ways of going about this. (1) Possible trends are extrapolated using empirical studies that are based on social and economic indicators, various scenarios are outlined, and finally an assessment is made based on what is most likely. (2) The second approach depends on the idea of alternative futures. For this, familiar patterns of thought must be abandoned. One distances oneself from the present and from conventional ideas and takes unusual perspectives that are sometimes even contrary to fact. By overcoming familiar (sometimes also entrenched) ways of looking at things, one makaes room for new possibilities both in terms of one's own future and in terms of society as a whole. This requires creative and inventive thinking, thanks to which one can imagine things that one is usually blind to in everyday life. The question is: "How could the future look if this or that were done or happened?" New images of the future look at and interpret the world in a different way and steer people's decisions and activities in new and hitherto unknown directions.

Desirable and livable futures

We can also determine desired futures by examining people's values, preferences, interests and goals. If we assume that the future is malleable, then the first question should be what future is actually desirable. We need to ask ourselves what we really want in the future, what is important to us and what we want to avoid. Desirable futures are closely linked to people's hopes for a livable world. So the question calls for an ethical assessment, i.e. a judgment of what is right and what is wrong, what is good and what is bad, not only for the individual, but for families and the communities in which we live, as well as for society and the planet as a whole. The consequence of this is that we have to take responsibility for our own preferred future.

In future research, we need to deal with developments that must be accepted because they lie outside human control or the influence of design. On the other hand, we need to focus on the areas that can be influenced and changed by people, as well as on the unintended, unanticipated and unrecognized consequences of our actions and activities (e.g. consumption, travel and leisure, environmental awareness, etc.).

Taking into account the three future categories, in this work we are interested in people's view of the positive and negative aspects of what can or could be (the possibilities), what would result under the given conditions (the probable) and what the best case should be (the desirable). We therefore want to describe trends, clarify interests, recognize preferences as well as develop and evaluate various future designs. In this way we can examine current ideas about the future and derive possible consequences for society. These considerations are embedded in the context of human values, which serve to assess whether one or the other future appears to be more desirable. In the combination of conditions and values as well as the possible consequences of personal behavior, it is ultimately a question of selecting concrete steps with the goal of making the future as livable as possible for all people and for the world as a whole.

4

Expectations of the Future

In the Hope Barometer of 2019, around 10,000 people in fourteen countries on different continents were asked about their expectations and wishes for the future. Many people expect that the general quality of life will deteriorate in the coming decades. People in wealthy countries like Switzerland are more pessimistic than people in poorer countries like Nigeria and Colombia. Past and current experiences influence the outlook on the future. The widening gap between rich and poor and the deterioration of mental health are assessed with particular concern. In addition, social and environmental problems are exacerbated. Technological developments such as digitalization are more often associated with fear and concern than with hope. Overall, a majority of people especially in Europe believes that it makes little sense to develop society as it is currently evolving.

4.1 Questions About the Future

In today's times, the future is mainly viewed from the perspective of economic and technological development. On the one hand, certain trends such as digitalization and artificial intelligence are accepted as all-determining and as a matter of course without questioning them or imagining future alternatives. On the other hand, we are often confronted with future problems and challenges (for example, climate change, environmental pollution, etc.) which can frighten, frustrate and sometimes discourage us.

The key questions we addressed as part of the Hope Barometer in November 2019 are how do people see the world in the future, what trends do they perceive, what scenarios do they consider likely and desirable,

A. M. Krafft, *Our Hopes, Our Future*, https://doi.org/10.1007/978-3-662-66205-2_4

and what values do they consider important. These images and ideas of the future will influence people's expectations and hopes as well as their fears.

The focus of the survey is on the assessment of long-term expectations, trends and future scenarios. For this purpose, already existing questionnaires of the Australian future researchers Richard Eckersley (Eckersley et al., 2007) and Carmen Stewart (2002) were used. The survey participants were mentally transported to the year 2040. We were interested in their assessment of future quality of life, their long-term expectations in various areas (health, family, employment, environment, etc.) as well as their assessment of possible future trends such as the social impact of political and technological developments. In addition, they were presented with various future scenarios which they could rate in terms of their likelihood and desirability.

4.2   Future Expectations for the Year 2040

First and foremost, we wanted to know what expectations people have for the future. In the fourteen countries, people were able to base their assessment on the following question: "Imagine your country in twenty years, say around 2040: Do you think the general quality of life will be better, the same or worse than it is today?" (Fig. 4.1). Even if the values are not representative of the entire population of a country, interesting comparisons can be made and first findings derived from the data collected. The lowest values were recorded in Switzerland, Spain, Malta, South Africa, France and Italy, where a majority of people is of the opinion that the general quality of life will be worse in 2040 than at present. In Australia, Israel, India, the Czech Republic and Poland, most people believe that the quality of life will remain roughly the same. In contrast, people in Nigeria, Colombia and Portugal are more likely to believe that the quality of life will improve slightly by 2040. In none of the countries do people expect the quality of life to be much better than it is today.

In countries with a higher standard of living, many people fear a deterioration in the general quality of life. People in poorer countries, on the other hand, expect the situation to improve in 20 years. In addition, the population in some developing countries has been able to experience positive developments despite problems still existing in recent decades. For example, in Colombia the peace process to overcome the civil war between the government, the FARC guerrillas and the paramilitaries has resulted in general economic and social stability and a noticeable positive development.

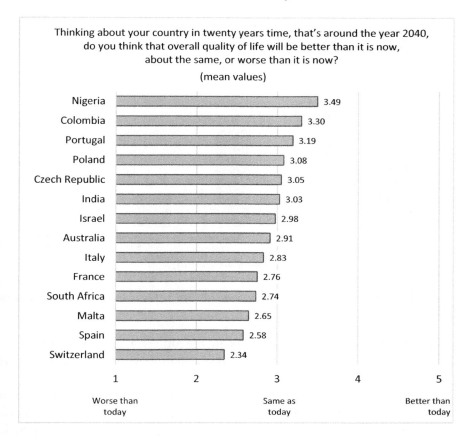

Fig. 4.1 Expectations for the general quality of life in 2040 by country (2019; N = 10,907)

It is particularly noteworthy that the population in Switzerland, the country on the list with the highest gross domestic product (GDP) per capita, has the lowest expectations for the future development of the quality of life by 2040, and that people in Nigeria, the poorest country measured by GDP per capita, have the most positive expectations for the future. In order to understand how these averages came into being, the responses of survey participants in Switzerland and Nigeria are compared in Fig. 4.2. Approximately 60% of the Swiss population is convinced that the quality of life in Switzerland will be worse in 2040 than it is today. Only 10% expect an improvement in the quality of life, and 30% expect it to remain about the same. The ratio is almost reversed in Nigeria, where 63% of those surveyed expect the quality of life to be better in 2040. Some of these differences can be explained by a slightly younger age group in the case of

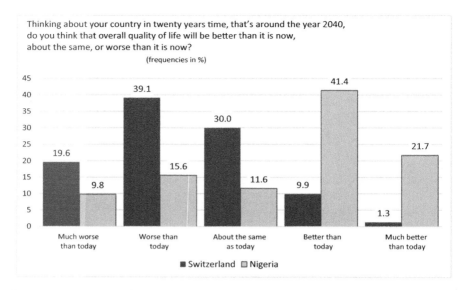

Fig. 4.2 Expectations for general quality of life in Switzerland and Nigeria 2040 (2019; N = 3935)

Nigeria. However, this corresponds to the different age structures of the population in the two countries and has only a marginal impact on the results.

In general, people in poorer countries looked more optimistically into the future than the population in richer countries. However, this should not obscure the fact that many, especially young people in poorer countries in Africa and Latin America, feel a general sense of hopelessness about the future.

When it comes to national and global developments in different areas of society, people's prospects are more likely to range from reserved to pessimistic. In Fig. 4.3 the future expectations of the European population are compared with the assessments from the other countries. In most areas such as health, family, economy and environment, Europeans have worse values than the rest of the countries. The biggest concern and at the same time the strongest discrepancy between Europe and the other countries is the increasing gap between rich and poor. Using the Gini index, which measures the distribution of income in the population, Switzerland for example is one of the countries with the most even distribution of income. Against this background and the observation of current developments, the future prospects of the population there are the darkest.

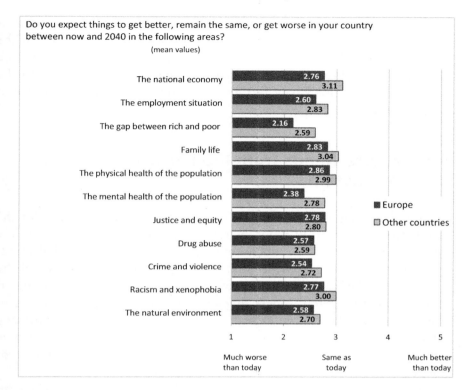

Do you expect things to get better, remain the same, or get worse in your country between now and 2040 in the following areas?
(mean values)

The national economy	2.76 / 3.11
The employment situation	2.60 / 2.83
The gap between rich and poor	2.16 / 2.59
Family life	2.83 / 3.04
The physical health of the population	2.86 / 2.99
The mental health of the population	2.38 / 2.78
Justice and equity	2.78 / 2.80
Drug abuse	2.57 / 2.59
Crime and violence	2.54 / 2.72
Racism and xenophobia	2.77 / 3.00
The natural environment	2.58 / 2.70

■ Europe
▢ Other countries

1   2   3   4   5
Much worse   Same as   Much better
than today   today   than today

Fig. 4.3   Future expectations in various areas (2019; N = 10,907)

The second lowest value refers to the deterioration in the mental health of the population. Here too, the difference between Europe and the other countries surveyed is significantly high. The perceived stress and the increase in mental illnesses such as burnout have reached alarming dimensions in Europe.

Another topic is personal and economic security. In some of the world's safest countries, the fear of an increase in crime and violence is particularly pronounced. In wealthy countries, there is also concern about a possible loss of jobs. Let's take the example of Switzerland once again. Although Switzerland's unemployment rate has been at a low of less than 3% in recent years (before Corona), the Swiss population fears a deterioration in the general employment situation. However, the experiences during and after the Corona pandemic show that this is not the case.

In other areas such as health, drug abuse, the environment, xenophobia, family life and equality, people's expectations for the future range from more subdued to pessimistic.

Many people, especially in wealthy European countries, are uncomfortable with the direction in which the world is currently heading. At the same time, powerlessness is expressed because it seems that nothing can be done about it. What causes this discomfort and these assessments can be explained through analysis of further future trends from the perspective of the population.

4.3   Future Trends from the Perspective of the Population

Against the background of negative expectations of the population for the future, the question arises about the reasons for them. This brings us to the investigation of global, i.e. ubiquitous, trends of our time. Global trends are socio-relevant developments with diverse impacts on our lives and the future. They affect almost all areas of our society (economy, environment, politics, education, etc.), trigger fundamental changes and have long-term effects. In recent decades, an increasing acceleration of mutually influencing trends has been observed. These are long-term trends such as demographic development, technological progress, political framework conditions, economic prospects and ecological impacts (Graf, 2003).

These megatrends pose unprecedented challenges to our society. How can the well-being of the older generation be ensured? How can the costs of an aging society be paid? How can the ecological effects of our consumption behavior be minimized, or how can nature be preserved? How do we deal with the scarcity of resources? How can agriculture feed more and more people while promoting the environment and people's health? How can personal and digital security be guaranteed? How can healthcare be optimized? How can material wealth be better distributed? How must the education system be adapted to new challenges?

For us, it is not trends in the technical sense that are of interest here (e.g. what new technologies we will have in the future), but rather people's perception with regard to the long-term effects of trends on their lives. In the Hope Barometer of 2019, we used the questionnaire of the Australian futurist Richard Eckersley (Eckersley et al., 2007).

The results in Fig. 4.4 give an insight into how differentiated the population assesses scientific and technological developments. Here we compare the results from Europe with the values from the other countries surveyed. The development of new means and therapies for the cure of existing and

Trends that could affect the world in the coming decades.
(mean values)

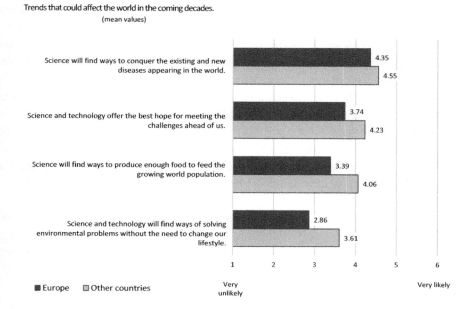

Fig. 4.4 Perceived future trends in science and technology (2019; N = 10,907)

future diseases is largely positively assessed in all countries. For example, during the Corona pandemic, we experienced the great hope that was placed above all in the development of effective vaccines.

Whether scientific and technological developments will provide good conditions for coping with future challenges by 2040 is assessed more critically in Europe than in countries outside Europe. Another concern refers to the question of how a growing population can be adequately fed. Remarkably, concerns are more pronounced in Europe than in countries more directly affected such as Nigeria, South Africa and India. For example, in Switzerland, more than half of those surveyed (55%) believe it is rather unlikely that science will be able to solve the problem of feeding a growing world population. In India, however, only around 38% believe this to be the case, compared with 62% who are rather confident.

Fewer people believe that we can solve environmental problems purely through new scientific and technological developments. Most of the skepticism in this regard seems to be shown by people in European countries, where awareness of the negative consequences of our modern lifestyle seems to be more pronounced. In contrast, about 60% of survey participants in Nigeria, India and South Africa believe that science and new technologies can solve environmental problems.

The consequences of technological development in the areas of digitalization, automation and robotics in politics, economy and society are seen even more critically in all countries (Fig. 4.5). Many people have a sense of what is wrong with this world. In the eyes of most respondents, new technologies will not strengthen democracies, but will intensify state control over the population (keyword "surveillance state"). In economic terms, increasing digitalization and automation will destroy jobs, leading to increased unemployment according to the perception of the respondents. In addition, there is a fear that new technologies will pose a threat to society by alienating people from each other and from nature. These are the assessments and fears of 70 to 75% of all respondents in the fourteen countries participating in the survey.

The results of our survey are similar in form to those of many other studies. Almost all researchers who have interviewed people in recent years about what the world will look like in 20 years and what social factors will

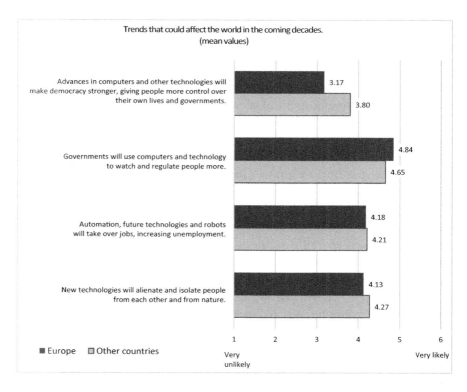

Fig. 4.5 Perceived future trends and their consequences (Nov. 2019; N = 10,907)

contribute to these changes have received rather negative assessments of the future (Brunstad, 2002; Eckersley, 1995, 2002; Hicks, 1996; Nordensward, 2014; Rubin, 2002).

4.4   Basic Assumptions About Society

In summary, all these perceptions and prospects regarding current and future trends can be traced back to a rather dark picture of the world and the future. Such images of the future are the result of partly unconscious basic assumptions about the world. We therefore wanted to take a closer look at this phenomenon.

To measure basic assumptions about society, we used Keyes' (2002) scale for assessing social well-being. The results of two representative statements are shown in Fig. 4.6. In most countries and especially in Europe the majority of those surveyed generally see little sense in how our society functions, and even more people realize that our society is not developing in an equally positive way for everyone. As a reminder, it should be emphasized again that these results reflect the mood in November 2019, i.e. before the outbreak of the Corona pandemic. In November 2020, when we repeated the survey, these values were even lower.

The key finding of the Hope Barometer 2019 is that people were generally negative about political, economic, technological and social developments (even before the Corona pandemic). The lack of belief in social

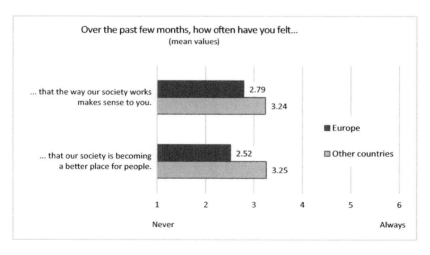

Fig. 4.6   Basic assumptions about society (2019; N = 10,907)

progress, i.e. in a better world, has led to a pessimistic attitude about the global future in many people. A large part of the population is disappointed with the economy and politics. The mood of many people is that we have reached a point in history at which things cannot continue to go on like the present: the exploitation and destruction of nature, climate change, natural disasters, social imbalances, broken marriages and families, and, equally bad, the exploitation of one's own resources and health.

Pessimism about the future is a result of increasing uncertainty and unpredictability. On the one hand, there is fear of one's losing hitherto achieved wealth. On the other hand, the inability of the economy and politics to offer credible answers to the challenges of our time creates insecurity. The more complex and incomprehensible the world presents itself, the greater the feeling of powerlessness because many people have the impression that they cannot do anything about it. These experiences trigger negative feelings of worry and helplessness. Increasing competition and pressure also bring dissatisfaction and discomfort. In an apparently uncontrollable world, it seems to be practically impossible for many people to imagine the feasibility of comprehensive positive change.

5

Possible and Probable Futures

In the development of future scenarios, four possible future images are usually distinguished: more of the same, technological progress, social and ecological disasters and sustainable development. In Europe, more than half of the population does not believe that current and future problems and obstacles will be overcome with economic and technological progress and that a new era of sustainability, peace and prosperity will begin. In contrast, a majority of people in countries outside Europe believe in the possibility of such a scenario. However, more than two thirds of people worldwide predict that phenomena such as population growth, environmental destruction, new diseases, and ethnic and regional conflicts will lead to a difficult time full of crises and disasters. These crises do not come from outside of mankind, but rather are caused by it and are the result of various long-term imbalances.

5.1 Scenarios and Possible Futures

The consequences of global trends and their mutual interactions give rise to diverse future scenarios. Scenarios are like maps, short portraits or stories about the future which take into account the trends mentioned above. In each scenario, one option or alternative development is outlined and evaluated. The purpose of developing scenarios is to design possible and desirable future images. These can be assessed as more or less likely and as more or less desirable. This process promotes open, future-oriented thinking in which possible consequences and alternatives are considered. Basically one imagines how a certain situation could look in the future by identifying and assessing possible changes and effects. As a result, positive and negative future images arise which in the extreme case tell stories of ideal and feared futures in the form of utopias and dystopias.

Experience from a number of projects shows that in their most general and far-reaching form, usually four typical scenario patterns develop (Hicks, 2003):

1. More of the same: basically, everything will stay the same.
2. Technological development: new technologies will solve the world's current problems and enable sustained progress.
3. Catastrophe: current developments will lead to multiple economic, environmental and social crises in the long term.
4. Sustainable development: new production, consumption and behavior patterns testify to a changed awareness and will bring about new social norms and structures.

In this and the next chapter we will deal with probable, possible and desirable scenarios from the perspective of the population which offer valuable insight into dystopian and utopian future images of society. In the Hope Barometer of November 2019, four scenarios were presented for the participants' evaluation by the Australian futurologist Richard Eckersley (Eckersley et al., 2007). Two of them could be evaluated with regard to their probability, and the other two with regard to their desirability. The time horizon of these scenarios is basically long-term, i.e. it is mainly a question of illustrating different ways in which the world might look in the future. The further away the time horizon of a scenario is, the less it is about a precise prediction of the future, and the more potential room there is for hope and wishes, but also for fear and concerns (Graf, 2003).

5.2   An Age of Wealth, Sustainability and Peace

The first scenario describes a positive development towards a world characterized by sustainability, peace and prosperity. In this scenario, mankind will be able to overcome the current problems thanks to current and future economic and technological progress. The participants in our survey were able to rate this scenario as more or less probable or improbable.

The results in Fig. 5.1 once again testify to the different perceptions and expectations between the two groups of countries. More than 60% of

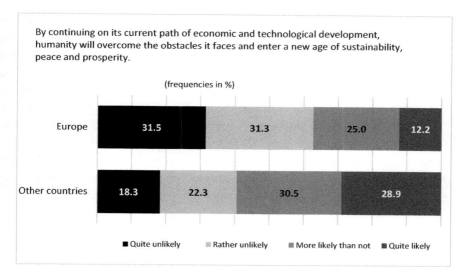

By continuing on its current path of economic and technological development, humanity will overcome the obstacles it faces and enter a new age of sustainability, peace and prosperity.

(frequencies in %)

Fig. 5.1 Possible positive scenario 2040 (2019; N = 10,907)

the respondents in Europe considered this scenario to be rather or quite unlikely. People in Europe (first and foremost in France, Switzerland, Poland and Spain) scarcely believe in a positive development of the world, which once again confirms the negative expectations and trends of the previous chapter. Poorer countries such as Nigeria, Colombia and India see this somewhat differently. Around 60% of the population in these countries believe in the positive effects of economic and technological progress with respect to social and ecological challenges.

These results can be interpreted first in a historical and cultural context. Since the late nineteenth century, a belief in universal human progress has flourished in Europe (and of course in the United States) and was further confirmed by the reconstruction after World War II: at that time, unlimited optimism and confidence in the future resulted in the belief that new technologies could fulfill all the requirements of society and solve its problems. Similar to then, authors such as Raymond Kurzweil (2005) see an era dawning today in which with the help of artificial intelligence, genetic engineering and nanotechnology, people can improve their general living conditions and further prolong life expectancy. In his book "Infinite Progress", Byron Reese (2013) describes a utopia in which the Internet and other technologies (e.g. genome technology) can once and for all end ignorance, disease, poverty, hunger and war. He derives this utopia from the rational optimism of the American dream of freedom and progress.

Between these almost euphoric expectations of technological possibilities and the attitude of the population there is currently an enormous, almost unbridgeable discrepancy. It is almost as if technology utopians were living in one world and all other people (in Europe) in another. Not only the population but also a new generation of researchers are skeptical or even opposed to techno-optimism and seriously question simplistic progress utopias. Scientists, philosophers and even former supporters of artificial intelligence (e.g. Bostrom & Yudkowsky, 2014) have already issued sharp warnings in view of the worldwide increase in terrorist attacks, military conflicts and nationalistic parties. The rose-tinted utopian glasses of technological progress stand in contrast to the dystopian images that warn of its dangers.

5.3   An Age Full of Problems and Crises

Most future studies show that when people are asked to sketch a picture of the world in 20 to 30 years, negative scenarios are expressed almost without exception. The second scenario in our 2019 study therefore describes a world characterized by crises and problems, in which a growing population causes more environmental destruction, and in which ethnic and regional conflicts as well as new diseases determine life.

As can be seen in Fig. 5.2, this crisis- and conflict-ridden future scenario was assessed by a large majority, i.e. by 78.6% of people in Europe and 72% in the other countries, as rather to quite likely.

The coming decades are generally seen as an age of crises and problems rather than one of peace and prosperity. The majority fears a deterioration of the current global problems in the future, seems to have lost confidence in a meaningful future and does not believe in an unlimited progress that could solve the problems of the world. This pessimism about the future is a consequence of the increasing insecurity. The situation of the world is considered by many people to be difficult, uncertain and out of control. Life has become unstable, unpredictable and inconsistent. The more complex and incomprehensible the world presents itself, the more difficult it is to assess the consequences of current actions. In an unpredictable world, it is practically impossible to change anything. The aforementioned experiences trigger negative feelings of fear, dejection and helplessness.

Particularly in modern science-fiction films, the future presented is often a frightening cosmic catastrophe caused not by divine forces, but by mankind itself. Sometimes such scenarios show an overpopulated and corrupt society that is characterized by unemployment, environmental pollution, drug

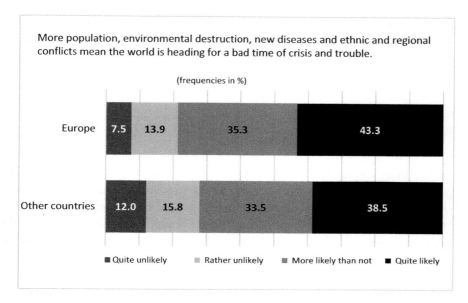

More population, environmental destruction, new diseases and ethnic and regional conflicts mean the world is heading for a bad time of crisis and trouble.

(frequencies in %)

Europe: 7.5 | 13.9 | 35.3 | 43.3

Other countries: 12.0 | 15.8 | 33.5 | 38.5

■ Quite unlikely   ■ Rather unlikely   ■ More likely than not   ■ Quite likely

Fig. 5.2 Possible negative scenario 2040 (2019; N = 10,907)

abuse, poverty and dirty cities (Nordensward, 2014; Rubin, 2002). Wars have left millions of hungry people behind, and global warming is also claiming its toll.

If there are no perspectives in sight, people take a defensive stance. One closes oneself off to brave changes and acts out of fear of losing the status quo, which results in increasing individualism and nationalism. Growing pressure and competition in schools and in the workplace also trigger dissatisfaction and discomfort (Eckersley, 1995).

The question, as Nancy Snow (2018) puts it, is whether we want to be a community of hope or one of worry. Snow confirms that the United States has become a nation of worriers largely because recent administrations have been unable to disseminate social hope. Our societies lack positive and generally accepted future images that can provide orientation and direction, as well as confidence and a belief that the world's current problems can be solved. Depending on how people look towards the future they will shape their daily lives in the here and now. Hopes and fears determine the perception of possible future states and options for action, and a lack of hope creates a society full of fear and worry. Only when new and powerful images of desirable future forms are present does a society begin to remobilize its creative energy (Hicks, 2003).

"We cannot build a future we cannot imagine. A first requirement, then, is to create for ourselves a realistic, compelling, and engaging vision of the future that can be simply told. If our collective visualization of the future is weak and fragmented, then our capacity to create a future together will be commensurately diminished." *(Elgin, 1991, p. 78)*

5.4 Harbingers of Crisis

Many people find the current moment in world history to be quite extraordinary. We are living in an exciting, i.e. tension-filled, time. As so often in history, it is about the struggle between hope and hopelessness, between new possibilities and old constraints and habits. Looking at history, we see that economic and social upheavals and renewals are nothing extraordinary, but rather that they occur at regular intervals (David et al., 2012).

Since World War II, two to three generations in Europe have experienced almost uninterrupted economic progress and, apart from individual fate, have hardly ever personally experienced a major economic, political or social crisis. Even during occasional emergency situations such as the energy crisis in the 1970s and the real estate and financial crisis in 2008, extreme situations were noticeably rare for a majority of the population so that one could almost speak of a "crisis gap" in comparison to earlier centuries (David et al., 2012). Since a major crisis experience is almost completely lacking in today's population, it seemed as if one could unconsciously assume that there would be no more crises on a large scale in the future.

And yet hardly a day goes by without hearing about some crisis or disaster in the media: environmental disasters, political debacles, economic and financial lows, streams of refugees and many other calamities are vividly present in people's consciousness. We are apparently living in a time of radical change, in an era of major technological, economic and in part political upheaval in the world. Previous institutions and practices in economics, politics and social institutions involving energy, transport, education, health care, etc. are in danger of no longer being able to withstand the challenges of the times.

In general, historians see the causes of most political, economic, and economic crises not outside, but rather within the common and successful systems and institutions of a particular time (David et al., 2012; Schumpeter, 1942; Siegenthaler, 1993). The causes of crises are usually anchored in previous systems and behavior, are often a logical consequence therof and serve to renew them. This is because every system, every structure, every institutional form has both strengths and weaknesses and cannot last forever without adjustments or changes. Here are some examples: the Reformation and, later, the Enlightenment were the answer to the crisis of the Catholic Church; the French Revolution was a reaction to the shortcomings of the clergy and nobility and to social structures perceived as unfair; socialism could arise because the imbalances caused by the industrial revolution were so painful for many people; the "green revolution" had its origin in the exploitation of nature; injustice and abuse have led to human rights, peace movements, equal rights for both women and men as well as for ethnic groups, and animal welfare, just to mention a few areas.

Crises usually arise when a certain equilibrium is disturbed. This can be the ecological balance in nature, an imbalance of income and expenditure or of give-and-take involving various players, as well as a disharmony in relationships. Crises are then nothing more than an indication of a disturbed balance and the attempt to restore a healthy one.

6

Desirable Futures

It is not merely current problems that motivate us to act, but rather positive images of a more livable future. Most social upheavals in the history of mankind were driven by visions of a better future. The participants of the Hope Barometer were presented with two scenarios that they could rate on a scale from quite undesirable to quite desirable. The first scenario of a fast-paced, internationally competitive society with a focus on the individual, asset building and technological progress is considered desirable by almost 60% of people in non-European countries and by only 36% of the European population. In contrast, more than 70% of all respondents rate the scenario of a greener, more harmonious society in which the focus is on cooperation, community and family, a more even distribution of wealth and greater economic self-sufficiency as quite (and another 20% as rather) desirable.

6.1   Positive Images of the Future

Future research recognized very early on that it makes little sense to focus only on problems. How the world will look in the future depends above all on how well we are able to develop images of a desirable future. What drives us are hopes and dreams in the form of positive visions and future designs of a livable world. It is human wishes and hopes that release the energy for a better future. The values and norms of a flourishing society are defined by them. The renowned philosopher Sir Karl Popper is reported to have said:

"It is not the kicks of the back, from the past, that impel us, but the attraction, the lure of the future and its attractive possibilities that entice us: This is what keeps life – and, indeed, the world – unfolding." (Karl Popper, quoted in Slaughter, 1994)

What drives history is human ambition to change a state so that it corresponds to one's hopes (Burke, 2012). Certain hopes are anchored in the culture of a society at a particular time. We see this in the dreams and yearnings of past generations for a better future. A sort of openness for something that does not yet exist, but could in the future. Bloch describes this cultural dimension as utopian consciousness. Cultural images and practices direct consciousness towards a desirable future that is actually possible. Thus, hope is an act of creating awareness that simultaneously works against alienation and ideology (Green, 2019).

If we let ourselves be guided by the ideals of social progress evident in human history for centuries, we need to connect individual goals with visions of the good life in a better world, and thus enable a new and more fundamental hope for happiness and fulfillment. Such a future can occur if, above all, we can imagine it mentally today and then realize it step by step. All the great upheavals in history, whether it be the discovery of America, the Copernican Revolution, the Enlightenment, the Reformation, the abolition of slavery, the equality of women and men, the emergence of human rights, the founding of the European Union, etc., are based on such visions, i.e. positive images of the future (Polak, 1973).

Positive scenarios offer people the image of an ideal future to which they can commit themselves, and they emphasize human freedom and dignity. Man is always free to imagine a completely different and better world and to strive for it. The goal is to deal with alternative and desirable future images in the conviction that we should not just adapt to the future, but must shape it actively and responsibly. For this we need future designs based on individual and collective interests, values and dreams of a better world.

6.2   Individualism, Competition, Technology and Prosperity

Hope for the future is to some extent a cultural phenomenon. Hopes are always embedded in social and societal relationships and in a historical context. The yearnings and hopes of people and of a society develop under the influence of particular historical circumstances. Societal hopes and visions require a process of value formation and have a history (Kleist & Jansen, 2016).

In the Hope Barometer 2019, the respondents were able to rate how desirable or undesirable two conceivable scenarios are in their eyes. The first scenario sketches a (modern) fast-paced, internationally competitive society with a focus on the individual, asset building and technological progress. The second scenario portrays a (postmodern) greener, more harmonious society in which the focus is on cooperation, community and family, a more even distribution of wealth and greater economic self-sufficiency. Following Eckersley et al. (2007), we want to take a look at what kind of hope underpins our society: hope for change or hope for continuity.

We begin with the "modern" scenario. As is clearly visible in Fig. 6.1, there is again a clear difference between the countries of Europe and the countries outside Europe. In Europe, about two thirds of the population consider the "modern" scenario to be rather or quite undesirable, and only one third as rather or quite desirable. In the countries outside Europe, the ratio is almost reversed. These results are a testimony to different economic and cultural realities, needs and attitudes of people in different world regions. It is perfectly understandable that people in countries like Nigeria, South Africa, India and Colombia aspire to wealth and modern technology.

The idea that the world could and should continue to function as it has in the past is seen as inadequate in countries like Switzerland, France, Italy, Poland, and Spain. However, this does not mean that economic

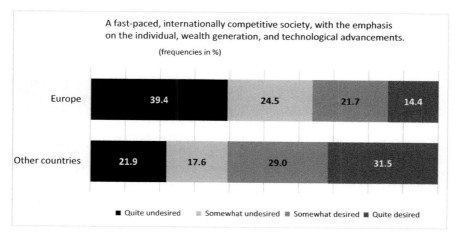

Fig. 6.1 Desirable "modern" scenario 2040 (2019; N = 10,907)

competition, individuality, prosperity, and technological progress are bad in principle. But these areas no longer serve as desirable visions of a better future, especially because their negative effects on health, well-being, and the environment are seen as intolerable. Many authors therefore conclude that there is a need for new social visions and better images of the future (Brunstad, 2002; Eckersley, 1995). The current images of a thriving economy can no longer offer people a higher purpose or attractive future scenarios to build on. Images of the future that convey only more of the same deprive young people in particular of their passion and enthusiasm about their lives and about the world as a whole. Having to look out for oneself leads back to individualism and selfishness.

6.3   Sustainability, Social Cohesion and Harmony

Most future studies show that people's ideals and hopes differ almost diametrically from their negative expectations. The alternative scenario portrays a (postmodern) greener, more harmonious society in which the focus is on cooperation, community and family, a more even distribution of wealth and greater economic self-sufficiency (Fig. 6.2).

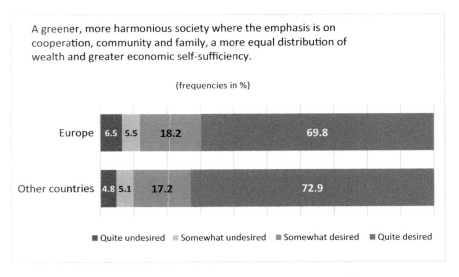

Fig. 6.2   Desirable "postmodern" scenario 2040 (2019; N = 10,907)

Remarkably, a majority of almost 90% of the population both in and outside of Europe agrees that this scenario is desirable.

Once people are asked to sketch their visions and hopes for desired future images, entirely different topics emerge in place of the previously noted material goods and technological progress. Some values seem virtually universal: altruism, generosity, forgiveness, peace, honesty, harmony, idealism and sustainability. In people's dreams, less emphasis is placed on the individual, competition and material wealth than on community, family, cohesion and environment. Most of all, people are concerned with natural, human and in part moral-altruistic aspects of life (Krafft, 2019).

The trend of increasing individualization also created a deep yearning for belonging and closeness. No longer a car or motorcycle on the highway (Route 66), but rather a house in the countryside is the new metaphor of the current century (Brunstad, 2002). The big wide world offers only problems, new media reinforce loneliness and anonymity. Individualization and the feeling that the world is falling apart have created a yearning for community, for harmony, for a safe place, for home, for security and protection. The ideal is no longer the traditional small family, but rather a large family composed of individuals of varied ages, genders, religions, nationalities and ethnicities.

6.4 The Power of Positive Social Visions of the Future

The results of the Hope Barometer raise the fundamental question of how we want to shape our lives and society in the future. For this we need first and foremost a shared image of the good life and of a livable world. We need not only short-term goals, but long-term visions for the individual and society. And we need clarity about what is worth striving for in life:

> "Beginning to see what is at the 'core' of life deepens one's understanding of the human experience. It puts the everyday in perspective, and hope partly emerges from becoming clearer about what it is that really matters." (Hicks, 2003, p. 73).

There is a need today for positive images of the future so that above all young people can think about the world in which they would like to live. Thinking about the future can open up new dimensions of meaning for people and give them orientation. Images of a better world can instill new inspiration. When it comes to designing alternative and desirable future designs, creativity and intuition and consequently emotions, values, hopes, fears, dreams and yearnings become increasingly important. Young people in particular experience the world less in a purely rational and cognitive way and more through personal experiences abound with feelings and emotions (Eckersley, 2002). The development of desirable future scenarios acquires a special creative value when current reality is overcome so to speak, and completely new ideas and wishes can be brought in (Bell, 2009). Hence the importance of hope and confidence instead of fear and discouragement clearly comes to the fore:

> "I no longer think fear is sufficient motivation to make changes … to spur us on, we need hope as well – we need a vision of recovery, of renewal, of resurgence." (McKibben, 1995, p. 5)

People will shape their daily lives in the here and now based on how they look into the future. What people do and how they shape their lives depends to a large extent on the ideas they have of the future, the goals they set for themselves and the means they use to achieve them. Hope helps to overcome fear and worry as well as apathy and depression because it inspires faith and trust in the achievability of a better future. This is especially possible in the context of a human community in which one focuses on the positive aspects of life, in particular on the hope and confidence that it is possible to lead a better life even in difficult times and despite problems and disappointments if one has the right attitude and is actively committed together with others. By working on new and powerful images of desirable life forms, a society begins to mobilize its creative energy anew.

Part II
Managing Crises

7

Causes and Consequences of Crises

Crises are fundamentally associated with unpredictability, uncontrollability and uncertainty, but also with openness to new things. They represent, as in the case of illness, a crossroad that can lead to either a negative or a positive outcome. Crises can be a temporary phenomenon or they can fundamentally challenge given practices and institutions. If crises persist over a longer period of time, there is usually a loss of trust in the existing rules and norms. Each crisis can be regarded as a danger or also as a valuable opportunity for inner transformation and renewal. Crises can sharpen the awareness and the willingness to develop new ideas and solutions. We have the choice of whether to face crises with fear and concern or with hope and a willingness to form and build a new. Fear and concern can shake us up, but also paralyze us and trigger false reactions. Through hope we can look constructively into the future and enable something positive to arise out of the crisis.

7.1 Trust and Uncertainty

What people feared about a still uncertain future at the time of our Hope Barometer survey in November 2019 unexpectedly became in part bitter reality a few months later. As if pessimistic expectations, negative trends and crisis-like future scenarios were not just subjective assessment, but almost prophetic foresight. Faster than expected, the world found itself in the midst of the biggest global crisis since the Second World War.

However, seen in a broader historical context, crises are not only something negative. The term crisis comes from the Greek and more or less means sharpening, decisive turning point and uncertainty. Originally it was

© The Author(s), under exclusive license to Springer-Verlag GmbH, DE, part of Springer Nature 2022
A. M. Krafft, *Our Hopes, Our Future*, https://doi.org/10.1007/978-3-662-66205-2_7

used in connection with the course of an illness. The crisis represents the still uncertain peak and turning point of an illness. The outcome can be both positive and negative. Depending on what steps are taken, the crisis can lead to healing and even strengthening or, in the extreme case, to catastrophe, i.e. death.

Societal crises are usually caused by a multitude of different factors. Economic, political, social and ecological aspects are more closely interconnected than we commonly think. The connection between climate change, natural disasters, technical developments, and the nature of global political, economic, and social systems is unfortunately still underestimated to a great extent. The corona crisis impressively shows how small the world can be and how strongly the global interconnections of economy, politics, environment, and social affairs affect us all.

Due to this complexity and dynamic, crises are naturally associated with a fundamental uncertainty and with a loss of trust in previously accepted assumptions, natural courses of action and practices, as well as in common conventions and societal institutions (Siegenthaler, 1993). Everyday life is full of assumptions and self-evidences that are rarely reflected upon and that enable a basic trust in the world and in oneself. But what happens when things and connections that one previously considered logical and that one took for granted, that one assumed to be just the way they were, suddenly lose their validity? In a crisis, much of what appeared self-evident to people until then is suddenly questioned. For example, an economic and financial crisis raises doubts about the established financial system, and a political crisis triggers mistrust in the political institutions.

When the world develops differently than one thought possible, trust in the old rules and ideas begins to crumble. The uncertainty that arises from crises refers to two levels. On the one hand, crises can cause enormous damage. On the other hand, crises confront people with a previously unknown and unpredictable situation and to a large extent challenge common ways of thinking and solving problems. The disadvantage of a crisis is that its course and effects can hardly be predicted. With some crises, one simply does not know whether it is just a temporary phenomenon or a fundamentally new development, a deep-seated change that completely throws existing knowledge overboard. It is disastrous to try to solve a completely new situation by traditional means.

7.2 Openness to What's New and Progress

Progress is often associated with crises. The scientific and economic developments of the eighteenth century furthered the French Revolution, which made it possible for a new political, economic and even social order to emerge. The same applies to the two greatest crises of the last 100 years: both world wars. Such crises often lead to a political and economic realignment and entail further social consequences. For example, after World War I, agricultural policy was completely redesigned in several European countries (Auderset & Moser, 2012). If you compare Europe in the twenty-first century with Europe in 1920, the progress that was unimaginable back then is clearly seen.

Every crisis can be a danger and trigger fears, but it can also open up new opportunities and give people great hope. In every crisis new possibilities for life are to be found. Sometimes things happen that we never thought possible and that force us to revise previous patterns of thought. This can help us to recognize and correct our mistakes and to rise above the problems. This is what we can call true progress. It can help us to improve both our lives and the world, which is becoming increasingly urgent and necessary in many areas (Hüther, 2016).

A fundamental crisis is an open situation that cannot be coped with by traditional means. One does not know in advance the course, the effects, or possible prescriptions for solving the crisis. Because the past no longer offers any support or orientation, one is forced to acquire completely new patterns of explanation and action. New paths and solutions need to be tried out because the previous methods for overcoming the crisis are unsuitable. In any case, every crisis can be accompanied by a fundamental learning process. However, this is only possible if one is willing to question what is old and open up to what is new.

New ideas and approaches can set positive impulses for a profound change of the whole world. Basically, one must endure a phase of insecurity and trust in human society's power for development and renewal, allow alternative ideas, concepts and options for action, and make room for new strategies. Ultimately, it is about leaving well-trodden paths and developing completely new ideas. Crises clear the horizon for new concepts if there is open mindedness. What could the economy and the financial system of the future look like? How must we build, produce, consume or trade in order to reduce ecological and social burdens to a minimum?

Confrontation with potential crisis situations should serve to expand one's own awareness of current events and of one's place in the world. Crises and crisis awareness should therefore not lead to pessimism, discouragement, dejection or even resignation, but should rouse and mobilize us. An increased awareness of current emergency situations and risks can unleash a creative force aimed at generating new solutions for crisis prevention and managemen.

Based on the Hope Barometer of November 2020, in the following chapters we present the key findings of how people have dealt with the COVID-19 pandemic and what positive developments have arisen from it. On a psychological level, crises are experienced in the form of loss, stress, uncertainty, uncontrollability and overload, so that we first deal with the perception of these phenomena. We then examine the coping strategies of the population that have led to constructive dealing with the events and consequences of the pandemic. We dedicate a separate chapter to the importance of hope and the essential sources of hope for overcoming the crisis. Finally, we show what positive developments people have experienced in terms of so-called stress-induced growth and what conclusions can be drawn for handling future crises.

8

Perceived Stress

In 2020, the entire world was confronted with one of the worst pandemics in recent history. Psychologically speaking, the consequences of such crises are perceived as unpredictable, uncontrollable and stressful, which are essential causes of stress symptoms such as nervousness, inner unrest and overload. However, due to their experiences, life situation and coping possibilities, people experience such events very differently. In November 2020, the stress caused by the Corona measures was examined in around 10,000 people from thirteen countries. Although many people, especially in countries like Spain, Colombia, India and Portugal, reported a very high level of stress, the majority of the population showed amazing resilience in the crisis despite the daily uncertainty and burden. Young people, women and single people felt particularly stressed by measures such as the lockdown, distance learning and home office, but were mostly able to deal with them in a positive way.

8.1   The Covid-19 Crisis

The years 2020 and 2021 will go down in world history as the COVID-19 crisis years. Almost everyone was challenged more or less severely by the pandemic and its associated measures. At the beginning of our study on November 2, 2020, many countries were in the midst of the so-called second wave of the worldwide pandemic. In the course of November 2020, a new negative peak was reached in Europe.

In order to contain the spread of the virus and follow the recommendations of the World Health Organization, many governments officially declared a state of emergency and imposed deep-reaching measures that were later lifted at various stages in different countries. Governments around the world have imposed widespread restrictions on daily life, including self-iso-lation of older people, quarantines of travelers, closures of schools, univer-sities and recreational facilities, and repeated shutdowns of economic and public activities. The rapid spread and consequences of the virus and the var-ious measures taken to contain it have placed every individual, families, the economy and society as a whole under an unprecedented burden.

The psychological consequences of the COVID-19 pandemic and the var-ious government measures taken to combat it are enormous. In addition to the serious economic consequences, these measures have had both immedi-ate and long-term effects on the mental health of the population. Relevant studies have reported a significant increase in stress-related health problems (de Quervain et al., 2020). In addition to the actual health threat posed by the virus, the lockdowns and the associated problems with homeworking and childcare as well as the social isolation over a long period of time were major causes of higher general stress levels.

Every crisis causes so-called stress-related endurance disorders and as a consequence is the source of phenomena such as worry, fear and depres-sion. Interestingly, not all people experienced these events equally. In a Swiss study after the first pandemic wave in the first half of 2020, about a quarter of the population reported no change in the stress level, about half reported an increase in stress, and another quarter even reported a decrease (de Quervain et al., 2020). Over the past few decades, there has been increased research on the role of positive factors such as personal and social resources in increasing resilience and constructive coping with crises. In addition, there are now several findings which indicate that for many people crises can act as a trigger for psychological growth. For example, during the pandemic many people found more time for new projects, for hobbies at home and for more physical activity, which at times led to increased well-being.

8.2   What is Stress?

Stress is understood to be a psychological burden that refers to an external state, emotionally affects people and requires them to make an excessive effort (Lazarus, 1993). Stress is caused on the one hand by external events or conditions, but on the other hand it is an extremely subjective phenom-enon. It arises in the interaction between external demands and the individ-ual's perception, properties and current resources and means. Psychological stress always increases when people are confronted with demands that exceed their possibilities and resources (or threaten to do so). Different people can experience the same situation in different ways, perceive it as more or less stressful, and also deal with it differently.

Stress triggers are certain external events and the personal perception or interpretation of these events by the person concerned. In general, stress-causing external events are concerned with three different aspects: (1) concrete damage such as the death of a loved one, a burdensome illness or a financial loss; (2) the risk or threat of possible future losses such as the uncertain future or the impending closure of a business; (3) general problems and obstacles that are perceived as burdensome or challenging.

All these uncertain and uncontrollable events are experienced through one's personal perception as more or less burdensome. This means that one's experience of the crisis is primarily an emotional reaction to the "objective" situation. The degree of stress experienced depends essentially on two personal assessments: (1) how strongly the situation is judged as being injurious, threatening or challenging, and (2) whether one possesses more or less inner strength to cope with the situation.

It is important to note that the reaction of each individual is not based solely on the intensity or some other objective property of the crisis, but is strongly dependent on personal and social factors. The personal evaluation of the situation is always the mediator between objective events and the individual's reaction to them. It is above all the subjective assessment and not the objective event that determines a person's reactions to a stressful situation. For example, the loss of a job can be experienced by one person as a threat to one's existence involving feelings of fear and worry, and by someone else as a new opportunity for personal reorientation that can trigger feelings of curiosity and anticipation of something new.

Many of the situations perceived as stressful are associated with the anticipation of future developments and events. Stress also refers to a threatening future, to a troubling situation that could continue or even become worse and which could exceed our coping skills. The prospective threat affects current conscious processing of the situation and emotional reactions to it (Baumeister et al., 2018): What will I do in the future? How can I feed my family in the future? How will this situation develop? In addition to current experiences (e.g. the pain of losing a loved one or pressure at work), it is above all the uncertainty and the uncontrollability of future events that are perceived as threatening.

8.3   Perceived Stress of the Population

As part of the Hope Barometer of November 2020, the stress level of the population was measured using the Perceived Stress Scale (PSS) by Cohen et al. (1983). The PSS is one of the most widely used psychological instruments for measuring stress perception. It measures to what extent critical life situations are perceived as more or less stressful. The scale includes a series of direct questions about the current level of experienced stress. In addition, other questions capture the reasons for stress, namely how unpredictable, uncontrollable and overtaxed the respondents feel their lives are. These three points have repeatedly proven to be central components of the stress experience. The questions are formulated in such a way that they are of a general nature and therefore relatively free of specific life situations. The PSS is particularly suitable for determining chronic stress under long-term life circumstances as well as subjective expectations with regard to future events or developments.

The ten PSS questions, which are rated on a scale of 0 (never) to 4 (often), are basically about the feelings and thoughts of the respondents during the last months. Thus people were asked how often they felt in a certain way during that time period. Based on previous studies, the stress level can be divided into three categories or norm ranges. (1) A low stress level represents mean values between 0 and 1.3. (2) A moderate stress level is characterized by mean values between 1.4 and 2.6; in this case, personal satisfaction and well-being can already be slightly to quite impaired. (3) A high stress level or stress overload is defined by values between 2.7 and 4.0; here the feeling of stress has a strong effect on satisfaction and personal well-being. A high stress level can seriously endanger physical and psychological health in the long run. The "normal" or common stress level in our Western society is usually around mean values of 1.3–1.4 (Cohen et al., 1997).

In Fig. 8.1 the mean values of the perceived stress level are presented in decreasing order for the thirteen countries participating in the survey. Since the samples are not representative, this is about a general assessment of the general stress level as low, medium or high. The central finding is that the stress values in all the countries studied clearly move within the middle range. Most people have felt a stress level up to November 2020 that is significantly above the "normal" level, but has not become a serious threat to their physical and mental health.

However, this should not obscure the fact that there are a large number of people who have seriously suffered under the circumstances during that

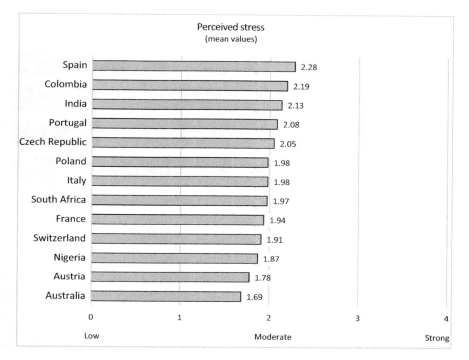

Fig. 8.1 Perceived stress during the Corona pandemic by country (2020; N = 10,002)

time. In the total sample of our survey, around 20% of the participants had a low stress level, about 65% a medium one and about 15% a high one. However, the distribution varies greatly from country to country. While in Spain and Colombia around 28% and in Portugal about 21% of the respondents felt a high stress level, in Australia and Nigeria it was only 6 to 7%. This again indicates that the events of 2020 had very different intensities and effects on mental stress in different countries and population groups.

To illustrate the type of questions and the answers given by the respondents, four selected items pertaining to the perceived stress level and the perception of unpredictability, uncontrollability and overload are presented in Fig. 8.2 using the specific example of the Swiss population. It should be noted that the values for Switzerland are almost identical to those of the entire international sample.

Just over half the population in Switzerland felt nervous and stressed during the last months of 2020. For only just under 20%, this was rarely or never the case. Some 37% of the population was confronted often with unexpected events, and a further 37% sometimes. This was rarely the case

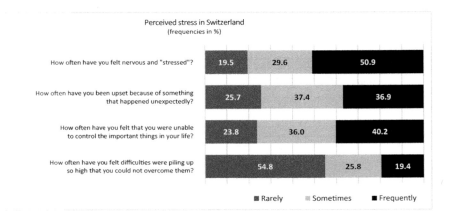

Fig. 8.2 Perceived stress in Switzerland (2020; N = 6968)

for around 26%. Around 40% of the people often sensed a of loss of control because they were unable to influence important things in their lives during the previous few months. However, just under 55% of the study participants rarely or never felt that the problems had built up to the point where they could no longer cope with them. This result already shows that many people had positive resistance resources and effective coping strategies, and were therefore able to cope well with the negative effects of the crisis.

A comparison between the sexes reveals that women in almost all countries (with the exception of Spain) felt significantly more stress than men did. The reason for this may be the multiple burden of women at work and at home. However, women or families with children – contrary to our assumption – did not have higher stress values than women and families without children. Above all, single mothers (unmarried, separated, divorced or widowed) between the ages of 18 and 39 reported a significantly higher stress level.

The differences are most pronounced when various age groups are compared with each other. Figure 8.3 shows how the perceived stress level decreases continuously with age even though in a purely physical sense, older people were at the greatest risk from the COVID-19 virus (risk group). This is the case even though the ratio of men to women in our sample shifted towards men with age. In the statistical analysis including all demographic variables, age is followed by gender as the strongest predictor

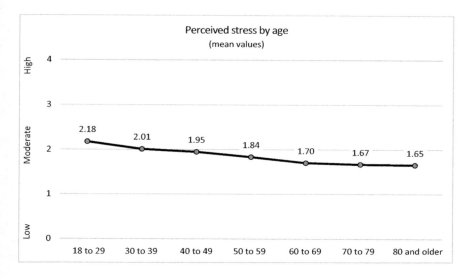

Fig. 8.3 Perceived stress by age (2020; N = 10,002)

of perceived stress. Young women have suffered the most and older men the least from stress.

There can be several reasons for this trend: (1) with increasing life experience, critical situations are generally perceived as less stressful; (2) older people usually have more material and social resources (savings, material goods, social network, etc.); (3) among younger generations there are more singles than married people; (4) younger people rely for their personal development more on their social environment, which was impaired during the pandemic.

9

Stress Coping Strategies

The ways and means by which people deal with a crisis is called coping strategies in psychology. Everyone has various possibilities and resources for dealing with a crisis. These can vary between problem-focused, emotion-focused and dysfunctional coping forms. The approximately 10,000 people surveyed in 2020 were able to use emotion-focused coping strategies such as acceptance of the situation and positive re-evaluation as a first choice. Using these strategies helped to solve unexpected problems and difficult situations through conscious and active self-control, planning and coping. In countries outside Europe, social support and religious practices were much more pronounced than in Europe. Women were able to react slightly better than men to stressful situations and to accepting support from other people. Only a minority of the population resorted to negative practices such as self-blame, alcohol consumption, denial and disinterest.

9.1 Dealing with Stress

Coping with stress is a dynamic process that adapts to new circumstances and influences the thinking, feeling and behaviour of people. A situation perceived as a danger can turn into a challenge if we accept the difficulties, look for solutions and handle them constructively. As long as something is simply perceived as a threat, negative emotions such as fear and worry arise, which can cause an inner blockade. As soon as the threat is re-interpreted as a challenge, new options are explored and solutions are sought.

The ways and means by which people deal with stress is called coping strategies in psychology. The word coping is understood to mean a reaction to relieve stress. The stress level perceived by the human being is influenced – as we have already seen – by two perceptions: 1. how threatening a

© The Author(s), under exclusive license to Springer-Verlag GmbH, DE, part of Springer Nature 2022
A. M. Krafft, *Our Hopes, Our Future*, https://doi.org/10.1007/978-3-662-66205-2_9

certain situation is subjectively estimated, and 2. what resources for resisting and possibilities for coping are available to deal with the situation. Stressful and challenging events are evaluated and treated in the light of the available coping options. The more positive and the stronger we assess our coping options, the less threatening the situation appears and the less stress we feel.

If we effectively mobilize and use our coping resources, previously experienced situations can suddenly be perceived as manageable challenges. Stress management means that we can change the circumstances we experience or the way we look at them. Situations that are perceived as stressful or threatening can be coped with by our attitude, by our way of thinking and by our concrete actions.

The way we deal with stress can be fundamentally of a cognitive (How do we think about the situation?), emotional (How can we reduce negative emotions and create positive emotions?) and behavioral (What can we do in this situation?) nature (Carver et al., 1989). Two different types of coping strategies can be used: problem-focused and emotion-focused coping.

In problem-focused coping, the conditions and situations are positively shaped by concrete activities. Thus the external conditions, which are perceived as stressful or threatening, are actively influenced by our actions.

With emotion-focused coping, the point of view, the evaluation and the inner attitude are transformed so that a certain situation appears less stressful or threatening. Thereby negative emotions such as fear and worry fade, and step-by -step room for better and finer emotions such as courage and confidence is made.

However, there are not only positive coping forms, but also negative ones. While, for example, the search for social support is a positive reaction, excessive alcohol consumption as a distraction from worries and problems usually has negative effects.

9.2   Coping Strategies During the COVID-19 Pandemic

In November 2020, we asked people about their coping strategies during the pandemic. The multidimensional coping inventory used in the Hope Barometer by Carver (1997) contains 14 different coping strategies that are assigned to the three categories mentioned above. In most cases, people can rely on all of the coping strategies. Problem-oriented coping is used when people have the impression that they can do something constructive to influence the situation and the sources of stress. Emotion-oriented coping prevails when people feel that they cannot take any concrete action against the situation at the moment, but at the same time do not want to be overwhelmed or discouraged by it. The third category contains so-called dysfunctional strategies that usually neither solve the problem nor lead to making the person feel better.

The 14 coping strategies are described in detail as follows (Carver et al., 1989):

Coping strategies

Problem-focused coping strategies

Active Coping
Measures that can change or mitigate a certain situation are taken actively.

Planning
As long as one cannot yet take concrete measures, possible strategies for action and future steps can be considered and planned.

Self-direction
One focuses on things one can influence or do oneself (e.g. one's tasks in the family or at work). This does not solve the problem immediately, but the focus is on what is currently possible.

Instrumental Support
This is about the search for concrete support from other people. The support can be of a material nature (e.g. money) or refer to active help in coping with concrete tasks (e.g. child care).

Emotion-focused coping strategies

Emotional Support
The other form of social support aims at emotional encouragement or personal backing. People need an open ear, understanding and human closeness in difficult situations.

Acceptance
Reality is accepted as it is, which is usually the prerequisite for actively and constructively dealing with it. Acceptance therefore does not mean that one resigns oneself to the situation and, so to speak, capitulates. The opposite of acceptance is denial.

Positive Reframing
A positive reevaluation of the situation takes place without denying the negative aspects. For example, not only the problems, but also the chances are seen in the situation.

Humor
The situation is taken with a pinch of cheerful composure. However, the humor must be healthy and not black or fatalistic.

Religion
For some people, the belief in God or a higher power and belonging to a religious community are valuable resources for coping with crisis situations.

Dysfunctional coping strategies

Disengagement
Disengagement is exactly the opposite of engagement and is an expression of helplessness and hopelessness. One renounces any attempt to change anything or to achieve specific goals.

Negative emotions are allowed and openly shown. Such a reaction can be useful for a while if the person feels relieved. In the long run, however, the negative consequences usually predominate.

Denial
Sometimes looking away can have a positive effect, e.g. by worrying less about the future. But most of the time, denying reality only creates additional problems, especially if nothing is done to improve the situation.

Self-Blame
In certain situations, some people look for the causes of their problems only within themselves and therefore feel guilty. Especially when self-esteem is low, people tend to reproach themselves ("If only I hadn't …").

Consumption of Alcohol and other Substances

When feeling anxious, worried, out of control and overwhelmed, people sometimes resort to excessive consumption of alcohol and other intoxicants. This usually only worsens the situation (one's own health, social relationships, etc.).

In Fig. 9.1 the mean values of the 14 coping strategies are presented for the country groups Europe and outside Europe. During the pandemic crisis most people have chosen primarily functional and only a few dysfunctional coping strategies such as disengagement, denial, self-blame and alcohol consumption during the pandemic crisis. Acceptance, positive revaluation, active coping, planning and self-regulation are the most mentioned coping strategies in both country groups.

In order to better understand how to construe these mean values in concrete terms, we refer to the answer frequencies of selected statements in Fig. 9.2. Three quarters of the people interviewed learned to deal with stressful

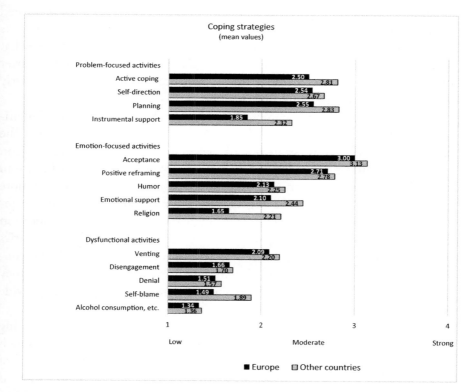

Fig. 9.1   Coping strategies during the Corona pandemic (2020; N = 10,230)

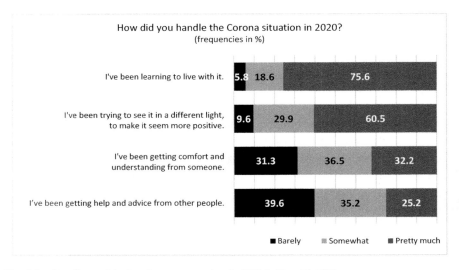

Fig. 9.2 Dealing with the Corona pandemic (2020; N = 10,230)

situations during the pandemic. In addition, around 60% have looked at things from a more positive perspective. As far as emotional support is concerned, in our sample approximately one third felt hardly, somewhat or quite comforted and understood by another person. About one quarter of the people interviewed (especially in non-European countries) regularly sought help and advice from other people.

A look at the different coping styles in Fig. 9.1 reveals some similarities as well as notable differences between the two groups of countries. The emotion-focused coping strategies of acceptance and positive revaluation were prominently preferred by both groups of countries. In non-European countries, people apparently engaged more actively (or had to engage more actively) as evidenced by the higher values for coping actively and planning future activities. The significantly higher values may be an indication of the greater involvement of people in these countries. People in countries like Colombia and India probably had to deal more actively with the consequences of the crisis and look for individual solutions, especially if they themselves had few financial reserves and the state was hardly able to provide resources for hardship cases.

Particularly striking are the significant differences in the social coping strategies. People in non-European countries could or had to rely much more intensively on the practical (instrumental) and emotional support of other people. Whether in financial matters, in everyday activities such as shopping and caring for older people and children, or as emotional support in difficult situations through personal involvement and availability, mutual help was much more pronounced in countries outside Europe for cultural reasons or of necessity. This also applies to the field of religion. Religious or spiritual belief and membership in a religious community were valuable resources for coping with the crisis in countries such as Nigeria, South Africa, India and Colombia. Emotional reactions also included increased self-blame, which clearly has a negative effect on stress levels.

The next question is: did men and women deal differently with the stress they experienced? The answer is yes and no. Men and women accepted the current situation nearly to an equal extent, and both genders went about solving impending problems and challenges actively or planned further activities with engagement. The essential differences relate to the emotion-focused coping forms. Women more often than men saw the experienced situations in a more positive light, and they also accepted practical and emotional support from other people to a greater extent. A religious belief and a community of faith were also more important for women than for men. In addition, women were somewhat more often able to let off steam and express their negative emotions such as feeling frustrated, overwhelmed, worried, etc.

9.3   Coping Strategies and Stress Perception

The importance and effectiveness of emotion-focused coping strategies could be substantiated by further statistical analyses. The relationship of the various coping forms to the perceived stress level is shown in Fig. 9.3. Negative values represent an inverse relationship and positive values a direct one. Irrespective of country, age, gender, marital status, level of education and occupational position, a positive attitude and acceptance are the two strongest factors with respect to lower stress perception. The dysfunctional coping strategies such as self-blame, alcohol consumption, denial, disengagement and venting increased the perceived stress significantly and possibly set off a negative spiral in the people affected: the higher the stress, the stronger the negative reactions, which in turn led to more stress, etc.

Basically, this means the following: one can and must unabashedly recognize reality in all its harshness and at the same time identify positive aspects and new possibilities. Because many people recognized not only the burdens, but also the good sides or new chances generated by the situation and used them (e.g. more time for family and hobbies, the definition of new priorities, the development of new interests, etc.), they were able to

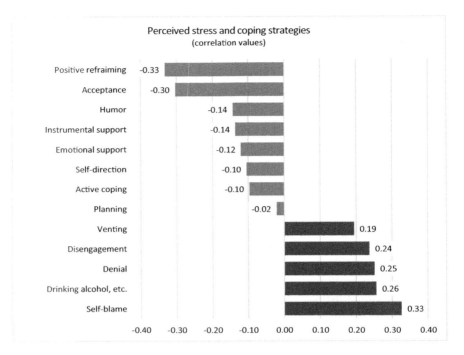

Fig. 9.3 Correlation values between perceived stress and coping strategies (2020; N = 10,230)

improve their attitude about the events and to feel the situation as being less threatening or burdensome. The depressing threat turned into a surmountable challenge that one could deal with constructively. Emotion-focused strategies are so important because they are usually the prerequisite for problem-focused coping forms such as engagement, planning and self-control. In other words: if we want to change a situation, we first have to accept and understand it, and then change our attitude towards it.

The connection between the individual coping strategies and the level of perceived hope, well-being, personal effectiveness and feelings of anxiety and depression (symptoms of depression) also illustrates whether people were able to cope better or worse with the situation. Irrespective of the country, gender, age, marital status, occupational status and educational level, there was a strong positive relationship between a positive attitude (positive reevaluation) and the feelings of hope, well-being and perceived personal effectiveness. People who developed a constructive attitude towards the events were also able to look more positively into the future, felt happier and more balanced, and also trusted themselves more. Similar effects were also shown with respect to acceptance and active coping. In contrast, anxiety and depression were mainly associated with self-reproach, alcohol consumption, denial and lack of engagement.

How stressful people find onerous situations depends both on the specific events and on their subjective assessment, as well as on the resources for resistance available to cope with them. In summary, it can be said that many people in our survey were able to deal constructively with the crisis. They accepted it as such, developed a positive attitude and were able to find active solutions for the challenges facing them. Only a minority developed more harmful behaviors such as disengagement, denial, self-blame and alcohol consumption. Women were able to rely more on emotional support and to focus on the positive aspects of the situation. Emotional coping through acceptance and positive reframing (positive reevaluation) usually takes precedence and is usually the prerequisite for problem-oriented coping strategies such as active coping, planning and self-control. Emotional coping strategies such as social support, positive reframing and religion are more often used by women and by people in countries such as South Africa, Nigeria, India and Colombia.

We ought not ignore a crisis, but also should not fall into panic. If we act as if everything is fine, we deny our worries and fears, i.e. we sweep them under the rug as if they did not exist. This can be helpful for a short time, but in the long run it can have devastating consequences. As a result, the causes of the crisis will not disappear, but quite the contrary: by practicing "more of the same", the extent and consequences of the crisis will be exacerbated. For this reason, it is important that we recognize the seriousness of the situation, develop a constructive attitude and take timely action to avoid and overcome the problem. As soon as new solutions appear, the threatening situation will be viewed with confidence again.

10

Hope in the Crisis

Hope plays a special role in coping with the crisis. Of the people surveyed at the end of 2020, more than three quarters said that hope was important for their lives. In addition, more than half reported that their hopes outweighed their fears in life and that they could remain hopeful even in difficult times. Unlike hope in relation to social issues, hope in relation to one's own life was above average in all countries. People in countries outside Europe (e.g. Nigeria, Israel, India, South Africa) felt more hopeful than people in Europe. With age, the ability to hope increases continuously. Although women experienced higher stress levels in 2020, their level of hope did not differ from that of men. The most important sources of hope were the support of family and friends, pleasant experiences in nature, and the experience of doing good with a meaningful purpose. People in non-European countries drew extensive hope from their belief in God and from prayer.

10.1 Importance of Hope

Against the background of the stressful events and resources available during the pandemic year of 2020, we asked people about their sense of hope. We wanted to know how important hope was for them, how hopeful they were, what attitude they took towards the future, and what gave them the most hope, i.e. we asked them about their sources of hope. What hope means concretely and what aspects inspire people's hope will be dealt with in more depth in the third part of the book.

Two validated instruments were used to assess hope: the Perceived Hope Scale (Krafft et al., 2017) and the Herth Hope Index (Herth, 1992). Fig. 10.1 presents the responses to selected questions about perceived

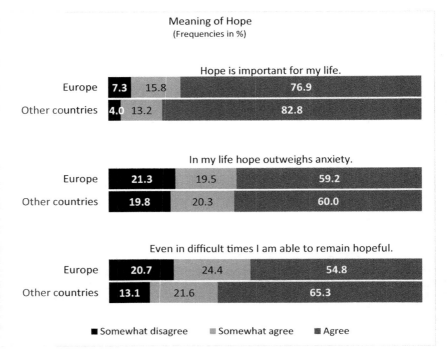

Fig. 10.1 The importance of hope (2020; N = 10,230)

hope. For more than three quarters of the people asked, hope was important for their lives. For around 60% of the respondents, their hopes were also stronger than their fears in the midst of the pandemic. More than half to almost two thirds were also able to remain hopeful in difficult times. However, for around 20% of the respondents (in Portugal and Colombia up to one third) this was not the case. This group of people was not very hopeful and looked rather anxiously into the future, which in turn was associated with a higher stress level and more fear.

These results relating to the difficult and uncertain situation at the end of 2020 are an indication of the great importance and strength of hope and testify to the pronounced hope of many people in the crisis.

10.2 Perceived Hope

How hope developed between the end of 2019 and the end of 2020 and which countries were particularly hopeful can be seen in the following Fig. 10.2. On a scale of 0 (not at all) to 5 (completely), all countries had

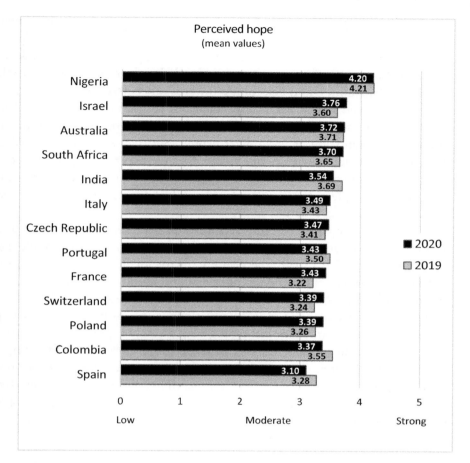

Fig. 10.2 Perceived hope 2019–2020 by country (N = 10,230 and N = 10,907)

an average value of perceived hope between 3 (rather hopeful) and 4 (quite hopeful). Specifically, around 70% of respondents felt moderate to strong hope in 2020. The highest hope values were recorded in Nigeria, Israel, Australia, South Africa and India, and the lowest in Spain, Colombia, Poland and Switzerland. Compared to 2019, at the end of 2020 people in the Czech Republic, Italy, South Africa, Australia and Nigeria had similar values for hope, France, Switzerland, Poland and Israel had slightly higher ones, and Spain, Colombia, India and Portugal had slightly lower ones. However, these results should only be considered as a rough estimate and not as representative.

While no significant differences were found between men and women in terms of stress levels despite the fact that women were under greater stress, age and family status were the two key demographic variables (predictors) in relation to hope. Women had significantly higher stress levels than men, but thanks to stronger coping resources such as positive reframing (positive reevaluation), self-control and emotional support, they were able to maintain hope. In addition, women reported significantly more noticeable changes in friendliness and helpfulness towards others (see Chap. 11).

As can be seen in Fig. 10.3, hope increases continuously with age. This result may also seem paradoxical since in 2020 older people were more at risk from the pandemic than younger people. But that is not the case. With age, health risks may increase, but so too does life experience, personal ability, coping ability and, as a result, a positive outlook on the future. In addition, young people suffered more from the lockdowns and the associated social distancing and isolation.

Age is one component, family relationships are the other. Married and widowed people are generally more hopeful than single people. While age (or life experience) is usually the deciding factor for hope in widowed people, married people enjoy the caring social and emotional support of their partner and family. Hope is particularly strong in families with children.

The importance of hope in crisis situations is shown by the relationship between hope and strategies for coping with stress. In general, hope correlates strongly with negative feelings of anxiety and worry. Therefore, hopeful people more often choose constructive coping strategies such as positive reframing, acceptance, active coping and planning, and much less often dysfunctional strategies such as disengagement, self-blame, denial and alcohol consumption, which have a positive connection with anxiety and worry.

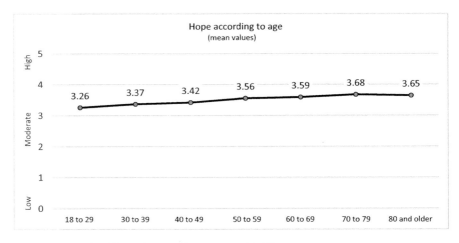

Fig. 10.3 Perceived hope by age (2020; N = 10,230)

10.3 Sources of Hope

In November 2020, we also wanted to find out what experiences during the pandemic particularly strengthened people's hope. The sources of hope are generally personal abilities, social relationships, positive experiences and religious or spiritual belief (Krafft, 2019; Krafft & Walker, 2018).

In Fig. 10.4, the support of family and friends as well as beautiful experiences in nature clearly stand out. During the lockdown many people in Europe once again experienced what a great source of strength nature is with its lakes, mountains, forests and meadows. In nature, many people found peace and a connection to a greater whole. At the same time, most people became even more aware of how important social relationships, in particular with family and closest friends, are in life.

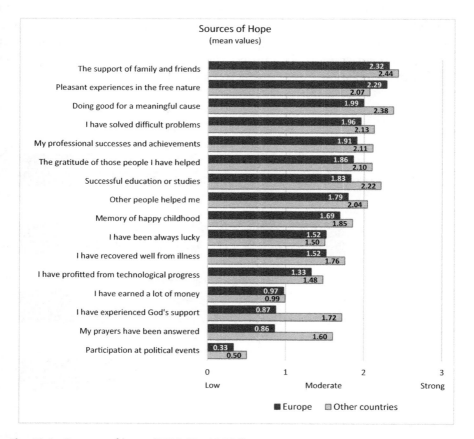

Fig. 10.4   Sources of hope (2020; N = 10,230)

The sources of hope that appear next are personal abilities and positive experiences related to helpfulness, good deeds and gratitude. Money, religious experiences and political engagement are of less importance (as in previous years). However, this does not mean that money is unimportant. Compared to other sources of hope, money is of secondary importance. In countries outside Europe, for example, people experience the value of good deeds for a meaningful purpose as well as successful training or completion of study as more important sources of hope.

Two essential aspects of hope, which are explained in more detail especially in Chap. 13, are personal attitude as well as belief and trust. The results in Fig. 10.5show how positive the inner attitude and how strong the trust of the person questioned is expressed. Just under 79% of people in Europe and 89% of those outside Europe feel a deep inner strength. Likewise, a large majority has a positive attitude towards life and can see new possibilities even in difficult times. In the countries outside Europe, in particular in Africa and India, people draw hope from their religious beliefs. Three quarters of people outside Europe have a strong belief or inner trust that gives them comfort. In Europe, this is felt by only slightly more than half of the population.

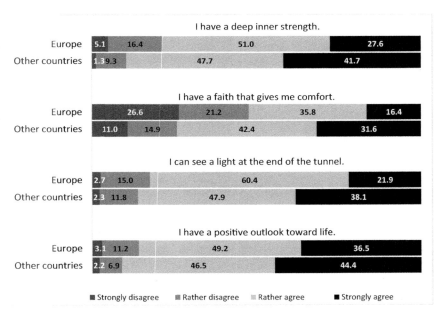

Fig. 10.5 Basic attitude and self-image (2020; N = 10,230)

In many conversations and interviews, we were often confronted with the assumption that people's hope ought to have declined in 2020. However, this assumption did not always hold true. In coping with diverse family and professional challenges, most people rarely lost hope. The majority maintained more hopes than fears and were able to remain hopeful even in difficult times.

However, hope is neither blind optimism nor a fatalistic attitude. Hope is not simply a good feeling, but rather a positive attitude with respect to the future. With full awareness of the difficulties and obstacles, hope is the desire for a better future coupled with a belief in future possibilities and trust both in one's own abilities and in the help and resources of others.

Even if it seems paradoxical: in crisis situations, hope is particularly valuable and pronounced. Often only in a crisis or in a difficult situation do we humans begin to hope consciously. Thanks to their inner strength and good social relationships, people can see new possibilities for the future even in difficult times. Thus, hope is a personal attitude that the human being can adopt on the basis of his own possibilities. And what is especially important: hope is not only important for the future, but it also improves the quality of life in our current uncertain and stressful times.

11

Stress-Related Growth

People who have successfully coped with a stressful situation in life can experience the phenomenon of personal growth through the challenges they have mastered. In addition to the many burdens and annoyances as a result of the Corona pandemic, many people have also had any number of positive experiences. They have come to know themselves and their strengths better and have gained more self-confidence as a result. In many cases, the caring and helpful treatment of other people infused social relationships with a new quality. One recognized how important it is to be able to rely on the support of other people and for oneself to be there for others. Many people, especially in non-European countries, developed a sense of social belonging and a grateful appreciation of the many small, good things in life. It is this kind of experience that makes us hopeful and leads us to look towards the future with optimism.

11.1 Areas of Inner Growth

Most surveys and studies on the effects of critical life events, including those in connection with the COVID-19 pandemic, have focused primarily on their negative consequences, e.g. physical and mental illness. Crisis situations have both a direct and an indirect impact on people (Collins et al., 1990). The direct effects are primarily negative because they trigger feelings of vulnerability, threat, loss, overstrain, fear and worry. The indirect effects take place through the person's reaction to the event and can also lead to positive results such as the recognition of personal strengths or the appreciation of social relationships. Growth under stress arises from coping with stressful life events.

A. M. Krafft, *Our Hopes, Our Future*, https://doi.org/10.1007/978-3-662-66205-2_11

The idea that people can have positive experiences and grow as a result of stressful events has been empirically confirmed several times in recent years (Tedeschi & Calhoun, 1995). Stress-related growth occurs primarily when people are able to deal constructively with stressful events. Stress-related growth describes the experiences of people whose development in at least some respects surpasses the state they were in before the stressful event occurred. The person has not only adapted, but also revealed significant personal changes that go beyond the previous status quo. This growth is not just a return to the same level as before, but the experience of a positive development that for some people can be profound (Tedeschi & Calhoun, 2004).

This kind of inner growth is not a direct result of the stressful events themselves, but rather a result of personally dealing and actively engaging with the events. Previous studies have shown that stress-related growth is most likely to occur when people a) experience a very stressful event, b) have a high level of personal and social resources, and c) use constructive coping strategies (Ameli et al., 2001).

On the basis of their studies Tedeschi and Calhoun (1996, 2004) were able to identify five areas of growth after a stressful situation and described them as follows:

1. *Personal strength and self-perception:* People feel stronger and more confident because they know they can deal with difficult situations; they feel more experienced; sometimes they also feel that they have grown and matured internally.
2. *Relationships with other people:* The person recognizes how important and valuable social relationships are; the relationship with family members becomes deeper and more intimate; the person can enter into closer and more empathetic relationships with other people; the person feels more sensitive and empathetic with respect to others; the willingness to help and accept help increases.
3. *New possibilities:* New priorities are set in life; one recognizes what is really important and valuable in life; new interests develop; new ways and perspectives open up in life; life takes on a new direction; one wants to do more good in life and change things positively.
4. *Appreciation of life and new life philosophy:* Life is viewed with different eyes; a new awareness develops and every day is experienced more consciously; it becomes clear how valuable life is; one feels gratitude for the many small and big things in life; life is taken with more ease; one enjoys every moment and appreciaates what one has.

5. *Spiritual Growth:* One's own religious beliefs are strengthened; one develops more interest and understanding in spiritual matters; there is more engagement with existential questions.

11.2 Stress-Related Growth During the COVID-19 Pandemic

In our November 2020 study, we used the Stress-Related Growth Questionnaire by Ameli et al. (2001) to examine both positive and negative impacts during the pandemic in the areas of self-perception, dealing with other people, personal strengths, optimism, dealing with one's own emotions (affect regulation), belonging to a community, and religiosity.

Areas of stress-related growth

Self-Understanding
You accept yourself as you are and are less influenced by external opinions and expectations.

Treatment of others
You meet other people in a more friendly way, respect their feelings and beliefs, and help them in need.

Personal Strengths
The belief in one's own strengths, skills and abilities is strengthened, trust in oneself increases, and one can make decisions independently.

Optimism
One can look at things in a positive way.

Affect Regulation
One learns to deal with with negative emotions in a positive way, becomes less angry about things that happen to one, and is not irritated by trifles.

Belongingness
One understands oneself as part of a community of people who take care of one in difficult times.

Religiosity
A belief and trust in God or in a higher being increases.

The results in Fig. 11.1show a slightly positive growth in almost all areas, above all in the friendly treatment of other people, the perception of personal strengths, optimism and self-perception. In all categories, people in non-European countries reported significantly higher positive changes. The strongest differences are in the way people interact with others, in the feeling of belonging to a community and in the area of religiosity.

What these results reveal in detail is illustrated by way of example in Fig. 11.2. 45.5% of the people surveyed said that their self-confidence had increased slightly or considerably as a result of the crisis. 41.5% said that there had been no change, and only 10.4% said that their self-confidence had decreased. These numbers say nothing about how strong people's self-confidence actually is, but only whether people have noticed a change in themselves as a result of the experiences of the preceding few months.

In addition, 43.7% of those surveyed said they were feeling more helpful towards other people. Only 6% said they felt they were currently being less helpful to others. Just under a third perceived more positively that there were people who cared about them.

Every critical life experience not only has not only negative consequences, but also potential for personal and social growth. Stress-related growth is

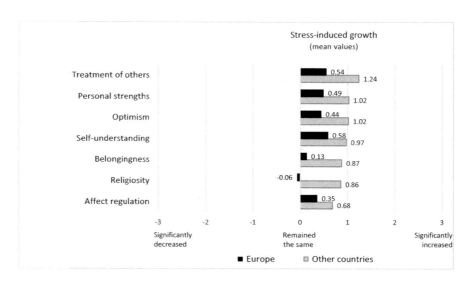

Fig. 11.1   Stress-related Growth (2020; N = 10,230)

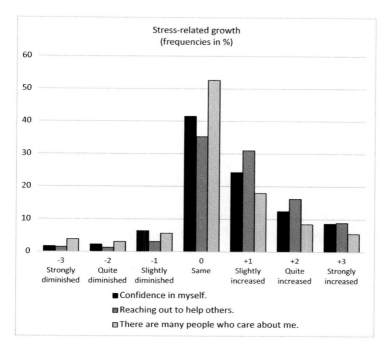

Fig. 11.2 Stress-related growth in different areas (2020; N = 10,230)

not merely the opposite of stress, but is rather a consequence of it. It is the interpretation and making sense of the new reality after a stressful situation that allows for personal growth. Only with progressive emotional processing of the experience can positive changes occur (Linley & Joseph, 2011). The positive consequences of stress are more pronounced the more the person positively evaluates and actively copes with the event. Especially when people do not lose hope for the future and use positive coping strategies, they can improve their own situation and grow internally. Even during the COVID-19 pandemic many people got to know themselves better, developed a friendly and helpful way of dealing with other people, and discovered new personal strengths.

A similar change in people's minds is also shown in a study by the Swiss Competence Center FORS (Refle et al., 2020) in spring of 2021. For many people the world after the pandemic is no longer the same. Many of them have different priorities after the pandemic. They want a different life and do not want to go back to the old normality. Some people have become more religious, others have reoriented their lives or changed their profession, and some have even founded their own company. People who were hard hit by the pandemic and lost their jobs have developed a different idea of what defines a good life.

11.3 Insights from the Crisis

The Corona pandemic has put people worldwide to a moderate stress test. This is by no means to belittle the far-reaching changes in the lives of many people and the sometimes profound consequences. Of course, millions of people (up to one third of the population in some countries) have suffered greatly under the given circumstances. The death of relatives, loss of income, social separation and much more have hit many people hard. We are aware of these fates, and they have also been duly highlighted in the media. Many of these people have needed concrete material, social and even psychological help. The values and resilience of our society are reflected in the extent to which needy people receive the empathy, solidarity and support they need, whether from the state or from their personal, professional and social environment.

Particular attention should be paid to a little-noticed finding. Even though a large part of the population reported moderate to high stress levels, many people were able to deal constructively with the burdens, difficulties and uncertainties in their environment. Especially people who could fall back on robust social relationships (family, friends, etc.) were able to cope relatively well with the general stress. Older people in particular were able to deal with the stress better than younger people due to their life experience and their coping resources. This indicates good resilience in large parts of the population. Most people experienced a crisis like the one of 2020 and 2021 for the first time in their lives. But many also experienced that they are quite capable of coping well with such challenging situations.

As long as one is in the middle of the crisis, the situation is experienced as frightening and partly depressing. In particular, if one has no experience in dealing with crises, one feels overwhelmed and depressed. A better future seems far away or even unattainable. If negative thoughts and negative emotions take hold of one, everything around one is experienced as dark and bad. Not the negative consequences of the crisis, which were of course to be expected, are enlightening for us, but rather the strength and resilience that millions of people have developed in the given situation. In this respect, the Corona crisis can give us reason to hope. Most people were able to successfully overcome stressful and challenging situations as well as negative thoughts and emotions, and were able to create new perspectives for themselves and their families. What this takes will be explained in the third part of this book.

Most of the time, crises are a prerequisite for personal growth because they lure us out of our reserve and we become inventive. If something in the world changes fundamentally, a corresponding adaptation of our patterns of behavior is required, but we are only then willing to adapt when there seems to be no alternative. Most of the time we then have to try something completely new without knowing whether it will really work. This applies to both the individual and society as a whole. The most prominent sources of hope are nature and the support of family and friends. Here it becomes clear how important our natural and social environment is for our inner strength and shaping of the future. The use of one's own strengths and abilities to do good, as well as the experience of helpfulness and gratitude, are other sources of hope and the best prerequisites for emotional, psychological and social well-being.

Part III
Shaping the Future

12

What is Hope?

As in the case of fear and worry, hope is an omnipresent and multifaceted phenomenon. On the one hand, hope is directed at specific wishes and goals. On the other hand, we also have a general and basic feeling of hope in life that enables us to cope better with difficult situations. Through positive habits and practices, we can strengthen our hope. Hope serves as a foundation for personal willingness and ability to make commitments and take action. At the same time, hope is based on the recognition of our own limits and the need to trust other people. The six essential elements of hope include: 1. desire for a valuable good, 2. specific goals and ideals, 3. belief in new possibilities, 4. awareness of difficulties that arise, 5. the trust in one's own and other people's abilities, and 6. the willpower to overcome obstacles and to realize our hopes.

12.1 Personal and Social Hope

In the past few years, studies from all over the world have shown a large discrepancy between people's negative assessment of society as a whole and the positive prospects with respect to their personal futures (Brunstad, 2002; Krafft, 2019; Nordensward, 2014; Rubin, 2002). There is great dissonance between what people expect for their personal lives and how they assess the global future: optimism with regard to the personal future and pessimism with regard to national and global developments.

As seen in the first part of this book, there was already a widespread feeling of crisis and of the political and social perspectivelessness long before the pandemic. For decades we have experienced terrorist attacks, natural disasters such as earthquakes, hurricanes and floods, global financial crises, refugee waves and now in addition a worldwide pandemic. However, it is not only the events themselves, but the general helplessness and powerlessness that are characteristic of these crises. The experiences develop into a feeling of omnipresent uncertainty, unpredictability and insecurity because one does not know where the world will or could develop. Distant events have unanticipated local consequences and trigger feelings of uncontrollability, vulnerability and fear. We apparently not only do not know where we are going and where we could go, but are also in the dark about where we should go (Kleist & Jansen, 2016).

This general insecurity represents a crisis of social hope itself in that many people no longer know where to find new perspectives for the future of society. Social and ecological hopelessness involves a conviction that the majority of people will not change their behavior and show no care or responsibility for the earth. Hopelessness in this case means indifference and withdrawal. In many places there is even a lack of belief that action could make a difference, which in turn leads to necessary measures being taken only hesitantly (Kretz, 2019). Thus, hopelessness is both the cause and the consequence of indifference and inaction.

In order to achieve positive change, hope is an indispensable prerequisite for the necessary activity. It is precisely hope that can prevent discouragement in the face of collective discomfort, disillusionment, pessimistic forecasts and fatalism due to the seeming lack of alternatives. In many places the question of what is good is being asked more frequently and the desire for a better world has been aroused (Kleist & Jansen, 2016; Kretz, 2019).

Hope arises basically when circumstances are experienced as unsatisfactory (Lazarus, 1999). Uncertainty and insecurity are indeed alarming, but they are also a prerequisite for hope. In order for hopes for a better future to be possible at all, there must be a certain amount of uncertainty. We need to become aware of such uncertainty and show willingness to shape the desired future.

In the following chapters we will deal with the nature of hope and its essential prerequisites and sources on both the personal and the societal level. Based on a pragmatic perspective, we will deal with questions about the existential value of hope, how we hope, what we hope for, and what we need every day in order to achieve a hopeful life and a hopeful society.

We can divide the phenomenon of hope into three dimensions according to Shade (2001):

1. The general and fundamental value of hope, independent of specific goals and wishes. Hope is a basic attitude of openness and positive orientation towards the future which determines how we react to the situations and challenges of life.
2. Particular goals, wishes and ideals that we hope for and that we want to realize. Our hopes are the driving force in life and the motivational source for shaping a better future.
3. Habits of hope are the means and activities by which we realize our hopes and which strengthen our general ability to hope. These include, for example, commitment, creativity, perseverance, patience and courage.

12.2 Capacity for Action and its Limits

All our actions, everything we do, is consciously or unconsciously associated with the hope of success (Dalferth, 2016). Whether we bake a cake, tackle a professional project, get married, go on vacation or write a book, we do it hoping that it will succeed. Thus, hope is closely linked to our ability to act and is the driving force of our actions. If we believe that the fulfillment of a desired state is possible, we feel empowered to do something about it. Hope provides the practical basis for our actions. Because we want something and hope for it, we act. Or, conversely, if we no longer have any hope (either because we don't want anything or because we consider the fulfillment of our wishes to be impossible), we would logically not do anything. For example, we would not write an application if we had no hope of a job, or we would not want to get to know anyone if we had given up hope of a partnership. Hope is the prerequisite for any meaningful and goal-oriented action. We have all experienced how it feels to do something without the slightest hope of success. Every action then seems unreal, artificial, demotivated.

The value of hope lies in the ability to act and thus also in self-confidence. When we hope, we experience the world as open to its positive shaping and development and have confidence in the power of our actions (Webb, 2008). Hope is therefore about much more than just formulating goals and fulfilling wishes. Thanks to hope, we guide our abilities into concrete activities and also recognize potential for future development. This can be best observed in children: when they set their minds to do something that is particularly important to them and trust themselves, they accept failures as valuable experiences for the development of their own abilities.

This example shows us how hope becomes relevant above all when we come up against the limits of our own ability to act, either because we lack certain means and possibilities or because our strength and competence are limited. In such situations, we can recognize both our possibilities for action and our limits. We explore the possibilities that are open to us and find out what we can do with them, and at the same time we discover where we can do nothing or very little at the moment (Billias, 2010). Sometimes we can realize our hopes through our actions. In other cases, our hopes are completely outside our control and depend entirely on external factors and circumstances. Thus, when we hope we rely on external forces and remain dependent and therefore vulnerable. The awareness of our own limits and dependencies, in turn, opens us up to the need for cooperation with others. At the same time, in the very process of hoping we can develop and expand our abilities (Shade, 2001).

The phenomenon of hope is so special because, on the one hand, in such situations the limits of our own actions are shown to us, yet on the other hand we do not become hopeless or powerless in face of the limitations. The value of hope lies in the fact that we become aware of our limitations and are not overwhelmed and paralyzed by feelings of disappointment and discouragement. When we experience setbacks and failures, we do not give up our wishes and ideals, but maintain our belief in future changes or better conditions. In moments of failure or powerlessness, hope can lift us up again and make us receptive to future possibilities.

Victoria Mc Geer (2004, 2008) even claims that in cases where we cannot directly achieve anything with our own powers, we continue to hope by orienting our attention, energy and willingness to act towards the future and the hoped-for good. By hoping, we focus our senses on what is hoped for. With hope, we direct our attention both to what is currently possible and to what could be if we were to develop our abilities or if others were to come to our aid. We realize that what we desire is often beyond our current abilities. In doing so, we learn about our limits, but maintain our belief in the possibilities of the future. Although sometimes we can actually do only very little, our attention and energy are still focused on our wishes and the future.

Sometimes we have to be patient, can learn to develop new ideas, meet other people, wait for more favorable moments. By not giving up, through hope we remain mentally active and continue to work for our dreams and wishes. Even in times of helplessness, when we can achieve little on our own, hope keeps us going and mentally active. We do not give up, but rather stay focused on our interests, longings and dreams, and will act again as soon as it becomes possible. Through hope we learn to wait and at the same time imagine what we can do and achieve in the future with the support of others. Although when hoping we acknowledge the obstacles and limits of our own ability to act, our will and commitment will lead to revealing new ways to reach the desired goals with which we can expand our limits (Shade, 2001).

12.3 Elements of Hope

For many decades and even centuries, poets, philosophers and social scientists have been equally fascinated and inspired by the human phenomenon of hope. Hope seems to be an existential need in every life situation. Without hope, we would not be able to lead a fulfilled life. For Thomas Aquinas, hope consists of the spiritual energy and willpower that are directed towards a desire that is difficult but not impossible to achieve. Based on various philosophical and psychological theories, the phenomenon of hope can be traced back to six fundamental elements which are illustrated in Fig. 12.1.

1. To begin with there is a desire for a valuable good. Our values, yearnings and interests are reflected in our desires, which is why we can also call them heart's desires. Desires are the prerequisite for meaningfulness of our actions.

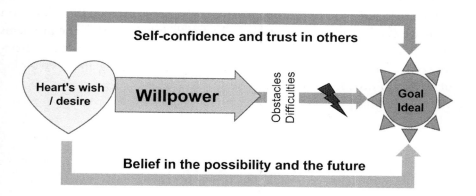

Fig. 12.1 Elements of hope

2. Wishes must be concretized in the form of goals or ideal states. Only when a wish is transformed into a goal can a person commit himself to it and orient his activities towards it. Without a specific goal, our ideas often remain simple wishful thinking. On the other hand, goals without a valuable wish are empty and meaningless.

3. Hope requires the belief that the realization of our wishes and the achievement of our goals are possible even if they are not necessarily likely. There is also a conviction that the future will provide us with new opportunities. Belief is nourished by our images of self and the world, by our beliefs and views.

4. When hoping, an awareness of the difficulties and obstacles that make the achievement of our wishes uncertain and strenuous is always present. Hope is thus anchored in a clear reference to reality.

5. In order to continue believing in our wishes and ideals in the face of difficulties and setbacks, we need to trust in our own abilities and/or the abilities and care of others (family, friends, state, God, etc.) that can make it possible for us to seize opportunities and fulfill our wishes despite adverse circumstances.

6. The interplay of wishes, belief, and trust in full awareness of existing difficulties and obstacles inspires the willpower to achieve our goals. The willpower with which we seize opportunities and use the abilities and resources to fulfill our wishes is characterized by commitment, courage, perseverance, persistence and patience.

Hope arises from a wish and the conviction that this wish is possible even if its realization is difficult and not entirely within our own power. Hope is therefore not pure optimism. In recognition of current difficulties, with hope we develop an attitude towards the future in which both the problems and the chances, the possibilities and the strengths are seen. Hope is therefore one of the essential prerequisites for the positive coping and overcoming of uncertain situations and life crises.

13

Between Hopelessness and Optimism

The value of hope is most apparent when we are confronted with situations of hopelessness, helplessness, and despair. Fear and worry can rouse people, but they can also paralyze them or turn them into self-centered egoists. Furthermore, hope is different from other phenomena such as wishful thinking and actionism. While wishful thinking suffers from a lack of responsibility and commitment, actionism lacks the awareness of the limits of one's own ability to act. With hope, we recognize our strengths and become aware of how important it is to stick together and cooperate with other people. Hope can also not be equated with positive expectations and unrealistic optimism. People do not hope because they expect everything will be all right, but because they are aware of the problems and difficulties and still do not abandon their wishes and goals. While unrealistic optimism can blind us, hope gives us the courage and strength to accomplish something.

13.1 Hope and Hopelessness

Hope is basically about how we look to the future in difficult times. The importance of hope in crisis situations can only be properly understood by thinking about the absence of hope, i.e. hopelessness. When no hope is left, people feel helpless and discouraged. The consequence of hopelessness is fear, worry, dejection, and despair. In such cases, the situation or even life on the whole appears to be meaningless and desperate. People stop hoping and abandon their wishes when they no longer believe that such wishes can come true. Hope is therefore particularly relevant when the life situation is difficult, when problems and challenges threaten to overwhelm us, i.e. when

© The Author(s), under exclusive license to Springer-Verlag GmbH, DE, part of Springer Nature 2022
A. M. Krafft, *Our Hopes, Our Future*, https://doi.org/10.1007/978-3-662-66205-2_13

we are not doing well. Hope flares up precisely in such situations so that we do not give up, but rather look ahead and seek new ways out of the crisis.

Anxiety and worry do not appear only during a crisis, but usually beforehand. Not just the crisis itself, but already the idea and anticipation of a possible crisis can cause people to worry. We worry when we a difficult test, when we do not know if our job is secure or when the outcome of a project is uncertain. Worry is often associated with powerlessness and disorientation. The more a situation is perceived as threatening and the greater the stress that is experienced, the more likely the initial feeling of worry develops into one of anxiety. If the situation is perceived as unsolvable or unavoidable, such worry gains the upper hand. It develops into fear and despair, and then into hopelessness and discouragement.

Hope is not only the opposite of fear and worry, but also the result of it, for in difficult situations it inspires a belief and trust in the achievability of a better future. This is especially possible in the context of a human community which focuses on the positive sides of life, in particular on the hope and confidence that it is possible to lead a fulfilled life even in difficult times despite problems and disappointments if one only develops the necessary attitude and works together for it.

Between the feeling of hope and the feeling of hopelessness there is a phase of indifference. One does not care about oneself, or about others, or about what is happening in the world. It is all the same to us what job we have, with whom we spend our life together, or who wins the election. Actually, nothing really makes sense to us anymore. One lives isolated from the world in a state of disinterest, indifference and resignation.

With hope, the challenges that lie ahead of us are realistically recognized and the measures required to meet them are taken. In a state in which faith and hope are missing, these measures would not even be considered. When a person constantly focuses on problems and fails to consider the aspect of possible solutions sufficiently, then a negative culture arises in which cynicism and apathy predominate.

13.2 Hope Between Wishful Thinking and Activism

According to McGeer (2004), the phenomenon of hope must be clearly distinguished from two other phenomena, namely wishful thinking and activism. It is often feared that hope might stand in the way of action because people would then automatically believe that everything would be just fine.

However, such a phenomenon would be a clear case of wishful thinking and not of hope. Passivity and indifference are not the result of hope, but of inertia and irresponsibility. Whoever remains self-satisfied and prefers not to participate in necessary changes thus reveals disinterest and laziness, or powerlessness and helplessness.

Unlike with hope, in the case of wishful thinking responsibility and the necessity to commit oneself actively to something are rejected. By relying on others or on external conditions, one remains distant and uninvolved.

In contrast, hope is an active orientation aimed at achieving one's desired goals or states. The work of Oettingen (2014) shows that dreams and wishful thinking only work if concrete goals for their achievement are defined and pursued (see Chap. 2). As long as one remains in a state of wishful thinking and no concrete actions follow, frustration arises. Wishful thinking does not mobilize, but rather paralyzes. No energy is put into the realization of the wish, and in the end one does not particularly believe in its fulfillment. In contrast to pure wishful thinking, hope engenders a feeling of empowerment and ability to act (Bovens, 1999).

At the other extreme, according to McGeer (2004), is actionism. She speaks here of a blind, compulsive and willful actionism that engulfs and limits people. People are so focused on achieving their goals that they ignore the existing conditions and use other people as mere instruments. Actionism is characterized by willpower and endurance, but in a selfish and arrogant way. The realization of one's goals is in the foreground, and this justifies all means, regardless of the undesirable consequences entailed. Actionism lacks reflection, flexibility and openness to the influence of external circumstances. People who are driven in this way show little interest and understanding for the wishes and hopes of other people and thus lose the respect and trust of others. Willpower alone cannot solve every problem; also required are the involvement and the caring of other people.

Psychologically speaking, compulsive actionism in the extreme case is based on a fear of failure and the need for self-elevation and recognition (Schwartz, 2012). Wishful thinking, in turn, is based on a lack of self-confidence. While with wishful thinking one underestimates oneself and is dependent on others, with actionism one overestimates oneself and isolates oneself from others. Hope does not automatically translate into successful action. We cannot always be in control, but must accept our dependence and limitations. We can hope even if we cannot achieve the desired result with our own might. Without question Self-realization and a sense of control and competence certainly favor hope, but hope does not always require them (Lazarus, 1999). The golden mean lies in a hope in which one is active but at the same time recognizes one's limits and can gratefully accept the help and support of others.

13.3 Hope and Positive Expectations

Very closely related to the phenomenon of hope are other phenomena such as expectations and optimism. Although these terms are often used as synonyms, hope differs in that we can even hope for things that we believe are quite unlikely (but not impossible) to achieve. We can still hope even when we can look neither confidently nor optimistically into the future. In contrast to positive expectations such as confidence and optimism, hope refers both to what one believes can happen and to what one wishes would happen because one considers it to be particularly valuable.

These phenomena have been examined more closely in new research projects, and it has been found that certain situations involve a complex interplay of expectations and hope (Cristea et al., 2011; David et al., 2004, 2006; Montgomery et al., 2003). For example, it has been recognized that past experiences and events have a stronger effect on expectations and a less significant impact on hope. One could say that despite past experiences one can have various hopes, or even hope for something new and unrelated to the reality of previous experiences. While expectations are often understood as past-oriented and future-oriented extrapolations, hope is determined less by probable trends than by personal values. However, this does not mean that expectations are "more realistic" than hope. In both cases, we are dealing with subjective evaluations and differing psychological mechanisms.

The inherent uncertainty that underlies hope contains a strong motivating force. As long as our hopes are uncertain, we must persistently work on them. Things that we already expect to happen, on the other hand, do not require any further initiative. The awareness of the uncertainty of our hopes also means that hopes are often more dynamic and adaptable than expectations. Hope is about both what we want to achieve and how we can navigate the uncertain path to get there. That does not necessarily mean that we always have clear ideas about how to achieve our hopes. But it does mean that we are aware of the obstacles that lie between our current state and what we want to achieve, and that we often have to discover and follow new paths to get there.

13.4 Hope and Optimism

The general attitude of hope differs fundamentally from classical optimism. Although an optimistic attitude is positive, it can also undermine the willingness of people to act because it does not take the urgency and difficulties of the current situation seriously. According to Dewey (1916/1980), American optimism promotes a comfortable and sometimes fatalistic satisfaction with things as they are or how they will allegedly develop naturally. The optimist sometimes takes on the role of the spectator who relies on a positive development. According to Kretz (2019), inappropriate optimism and excessively positive messages are just as harmful as discouragement and pessimism.

The person who hopes, on the other hand, plays the role of the participant who actively fights against negative developments (West, 2009). In the case of hope, current evils and problems are clearly recognized while forces aimed at eliminating and overcoming them are generated. While optimism claims "everything will be fine", hope remarks "we can improve something". The way in which we deal with the obstacles and problems of the world is determined by hope for a future with new possibilities. The hopeful person does not believe, like an optimist, in inevitable progress, but rather calls for action (McGeer, 2004).

For Kadlac (2015) hope therefore involves the following advantages: it enables a realistic view of the present and future and protects us from too much optimism or pessimism. With pessimism, one focuses on the negative aspects of a situation and overlooks the positive ones; with optimism it is the other way around. With hope, one recognizes the seriousness of the situation while at the same time developing a wish that one believes to be possible but not certain. It promotes courage in the face of an uncertain future and favors solidarity with other human beings.

14

How We Hope

The power of imagination, a belief in the possibilities of the future, trust in ourselves and others, and the motivating energy of willpower and commitment all reside in hope. With our imagination we can envision a future different from current reality and strive for it. The ability to imagine something that does not yet exist is a prerequisite for personal and social change. A belief in new and previously unimagined possibilities for realizing our wishes gives us the strength to commit ourselves to those wishes. In this respect, faith is stronger than the knowledge of facts. By hoping, we trust in the abilities, strengths, and caring consideration of ourselves and others. The trust that lives in hope is an expression of appreciation, community, and solidarity. Self-worth and self-confidence are linked to the recognition of our vulnerability and mutual dependence.

14.1 Mental Imagination

In Chap. 12 we said that hope consists of several elements: the desire for a better future, a concrete goal, a belief in the possibilities of realizing that desire, an awareness of prevailing difficulties and obstacles, a trust in the ability to overcome them, and the willpower by virtue of which we engage in achieving the goals. In this chapter, we will show how hope works and will deepen our understanding of the phenomena of mental imagination, belief and trust, as well as of energy, motivation and willpower.

When it comes to the design and realization of our hopes, our knowledge of what is possible or not often proves to be insufficient. Sometimes our wishes and projects are beyond the horizon of what is currently possible. However, we can imagine new possibilities mentally. In moments when we

© The Author(s), under exclusive license to Springer-Verlag GmbH, DE, part of Springer Nature 2022
A. M. Krafft, *Our Hopes, Our Future*, https://doi.org/10.1007/978-3-662-66205-2_14

hope for something, we usually develop a mental image of what it is that we are hoping for. The basis for our exploration of new possibilities is our inspiration and power of imagination. For hope, the power of imagination and the development of new ideas are important because they enable us to overcome the current situation mentally. Without the ability to imagine something other than what is the present case, hope would have no direction (Kretz, 2019). Thanks to our power of imagination, we can overcome current limitations and transport ourselves into the future. With our power of imagination we can think and go beyond what currently determines us and formulate new ideals and goals. We can play with our thoughts and imagine something different and better for our lives and for the world. With our power of imagination we design alternative future images and commit ourselves to them (Stitzlein, 2019).

For Bovens (1999), hope's power of imagination has a threefold worth. First, the mental image itself is already valuable because we associate it with positive emotions such as reassurance, interest, anticipation or inspiration. Second, the mental image expands our consciousness and our self-conception in that we imagine things that do not yet exist. Third, hope is also an act of love and caring, either in relation to oneself (as an expression of self-worth) or in relation to someone else (as an expression of love of one's neighbor). In thinking about the well-being of another person and hoping for it, we develop a mental energy that is nothing less than love.

The wishes of an individual can develop into collective social visions of how society might look in the future. According to Kretz (2019), we also need to think beyond what is immediate and obvious in our everyday lives for ethical reasons. If we do not think far enough beyond the status quo, we will not be able to realize the changes we desire and that can drive hope. A too strict focus on immediate feasibility can hinder creativity and progress.

Sometimes one has to break the common ways of thinking that have developed over the decades and have even become invisible to us. To have a better horizon to hope for, we also need better imagination. People's imagination expands through opening up to alternative ideas and perspectives. This shifts the boundaries of what can be imagined and hoped for. Moral imagination gives us the ability to tell a completely different story of what the future can bring, and hope gives us part of the required motivation and the necessary skills to get us there.

With concrete wish images and goals, we can maintain our hopes and align our actions accordingly. However, we also need to be open to new perspectives and not hold too strongly to a preconceived idea. Sometimes our imagination can also restrict and paralyze us. By focusing too much on our own thoughts, we can overlook other possibilities and ideas, which in turn can limit us. Hope often has to do with research and experimentation, which is also why we should remain open to new things (Stitzlein, 2019).

14.2 Belief and Trust

Hope includes the belief that something good that we yearn for can occur. Thus, hope is much more than just a wish. It requires a belief in the possibility of a favorable outcome (Lazarus, 1999). In contrast, a belief that important things in life are impossible plunges us into dejection, indifference or despair. With a belief in the impossibility of our dreams, we are not only separated from our wishes, but also from ourselves and in many cases from others. In hope lives the belief that we can overcome current limits, change and develop ourselves and the world. Despite difficult circumstances and negative expectations, in hoping we orient ourselves towards the desired event and act accordingly when an opportunity arises. Consequently, hope holds fast to a belief in possibility (Miceli & Castelfranchi, 2010).

Hope is basically related to a belief in goodness (Krafft, 2019). The hope for growth and change is based for Rorty (1999, p. 20) in analogy to Dewey on the "belief that the future will be indeterminably different and indeterminably freer than the past". If we did not believe in goodness, we could not hope. Thus, for Meirav (2009) hope implies a belief in forces that are beyond our control. In order to maintain hope, we must believe in a benevolent or advantageous external entity (nature, social support, luck, fate, God, etc.). Often, our hope depends on a belief in the goodness or care of such an external power. Thus in general, we trust in goodness in the world or, as Tennen and his colleagues would say (Tennen et al., 2002): hope requires a feeling of trust that the world makes sense.

Belief is a conviction not about how things are, but about how they could be in the future if we work at it. Belief and hope are not tied to any facts or probabilities. Hope is an attitude with which we express our belief in future possibilities and our commitment to their realization. For the American philosopher William James (1979, p. 76), hope means "beliefing in something concerning which doubt is still theoretically possible, and as a test of belief is willingness to act, one may say that faith is the readiness to act in a cause the prosperous issue of which is not certified to us in advance." In the activity of hoping, a certain form of belief is included inasmuch as we consider something possible and act as if we could achieve it, even though we do not know if we will actually succeed.

Thus, belief is not weaker than knowledge, but quite the contrary. It is the conviction of what could be thanks to our commitment and our ideals. Belief therefore requires courage in that it shows our willingness to stick to a goal according to our convictions despite current uncertainties and difficulties. Without a belief in future possibilities, we would not initiate or act upon wishes. In this respect, belief is a precursor to knowledge. Once a goal has been achieved and a possibility realized, belief turns into knowledge.

Hope involves believing in new possibilities in the future. Technological, medical, and social progress is evidence of this. What was once considered unthinkable suddenly becomes possible. On a personal level, we often find that we are capable of more than what we thought. The current limits of our knowledge and action are not set in stone, but can be developed and expanded. What we have not been able to do up to now, we can learn and then accomplish. Current facts give us only poor insight into future possibilities. The past and the present offer us an insufficient basis for imagining the future. So our current knowledge can both limit us and open up new paths. For the latter, however, creativity and "unrealistic" ideas are required for the development of new goals and options for action (Shade, 2001).

The belief that a goal is really possible is the prerequisite for confidence in oneself and in others. Hope is also based on a belief in the possibility of a better world and in the confidence that we can achieve it together. Substantial hope, as McGeer (2008) calls it, implies substantial trust, i.e. a trust that persists despite negative facts and evidence. With trust, be it in ourselves, in other people, or in a universal power, we can hold on to our hopes and continue to believe in them even when we are currently confronted with obstacles, difficulties and setbacks. When we hope, we basically trust that there are forces that can make the realization of our hopes possible.

As soon as we focus our hope not only on what we can do in a certain situation, but also on what others can do for us, we have to place trust in other people. With this in mind we rely on them, hoping that they will help us in this particular situation. When we put our trust and hope in others, we also extend them our appreciation (Martin, 2019). Hopeful trust works simultaneously as an expectation and as a gift. We expect care and support from others and give them a caring and helpful image of themselves in return. Our hopeful image of them inspires and mobilizes them with motivating energy and self-confidence in their own competence and willingness to help (McGeer, 2008).

Let's think about how it feels when other people hope for and trust us. When other people believe in us and trust us, we are strengthened from within. They are telling us that they see abilities in us that we ourselves are not yet aware of or that we do not believe in yet. This appreciation strengthens our self-confidence and ignites our willingness to hope. When others believe in us, then we should not disappoint them but rather start to believe in ourselves. The gratitude of people we have helped is an essential source of hope both for those people and for ourselves.

14.3 Energy, Willpower and Commitment

Hope is a motivating force without which we would hardly engage in anything new or challenging. We always hope, so Thomas Aquinas, when we direct our mental energy and willpower towards a desire that is difficult but not impossible to achieve. Hope is part of a positive, forward-looking perspective that takes current, sometimes burdensome life circumstances seriously but is open to future possibilities. Pettit (2004) refers to the energy and willpower contained in hope as "mental determination". This mental (cognitive) determination of hope begins with a thought experiment in which one imagines a "what if?" scenario and compares it to current conditions and beliefs.

Especially when a task is arduous, thanks to hope we explore how to enhance our abilities and exercise them in new and creative ways. In the act of hoping, certain energies are released and our abilities are expanded so that we can grow beyond our previous limits. On the one hand, hope recognizes our limited ability to act. On the other hand, hope mobilizes energies for the future. Hope means: "… we invest ourselves in developing a horizon of meaningful promising possibilities." (Shade, 2001, p. 69).

Even if we cannot do anything at the moment to fulfil our hopes, hope orients our willpower towards the desired state not in action, but all the more in thought. By hoping we preserve an active interest in the future and in its possibilities. Even when we can actively do little to realise our hopes, hope keeps us ready to act namely by orienting and engaging our thoughts towards a better future. This energy and willpower manifests itself both in the form of patience when we wait for a favourable condition, and in the readiness to take action when an opportunity presents itself. We can say, as McGeer (2004, p. 104) puts it: "although there may be nothing we can do now to bring about what we desire, our energy is still oriented toward the future, limitations notwithstanding".

Hope keeps our energy flowing and plays a decisive role in motivating action (Calhoun, 2018; Kretz, 2019; Walker, 2006). By always including a desirable future, it also contains the idea of what people consider progress as well as the assessment of whether it is worth striving for despite the uncertainty and great effort involved. People who cherish the desire for a better life also recognise the possibilities for its fulfilment and can break down entrenched assumptions and patterns of thought and adopt new ideas. Thus hope implies a strong motivational state. These properties make hope particularly important because they determine whether people are willing to invest in their future, in a risky undertaking or in cooperation with others.

15

What We Hope

Our wishes and hopes are an expression of our values, needs, yearnings and interests. Therefore, the first question is not "What can we hope for?", but "What do we want to hope for?". With our hopes we determine the priorities in our lives and decide what is important and valuable to us. People's most important hopes include good health, a happy family, marriage or partnership, harmony in life, good social relationships, self-determination and a meaningful purpose in life. Learning and personal growth as well as success, performance and career are of particular importance to young people in emerging countries. When imagining their best possible self, young adults in Switzerland hardly ever think of material goods and financial success. Again, values such as harmony, well-being, work-life balance, a happy family, friendly relationships and a fulfilling activity with a meaningful purpose figure in the foreground.

15.1 Wishes and Values

It is in the nature of mankind that one wants to fulfill one's wishes and realize one's ideals. Our hopes are always directed towards a desirable good. In this respect, hope tells us a lot about what people really want and what motivates their behavior. Most hope theories ignore the question of what kinds of hope people have and how they determine them. Often it is simply assumed that people have various hopes to which they emotionally and actively commit themselves.

Personal wishes and yearnings are defined in the light of our values, interests and ideals. Concrete hopes are based on what we consider good, meaningful and desirable in life. Therefore, our self-conception and our identity

© The Author(s), under exclusive license to Springer-Verlag GmbH, DE, part of Springer Nature 2022
A. M. Krafft, *Our Hopes, Our Future*, https://doi.org/10.1007/978-3-662-66205-2_15

are anchored in our hopes. With our hopes we make an open commitment to what we wish and desire in the here and now as well as to the desirable future life that we imagine for ourselves. Hopes give our life a meaning as well as recognize the obstacles that stand in the way of the realization of our wishes and desires. They are particularly important and relevant because they take us beyond the current limits of our existence and reveal new horizons. In the realization of our hopes, we expand our lives and flourish as human beings.

The question therefore arises as to which hopes people consider important and desirable. By asking people what they need, what they want and what their priorities are, we can focus on what is really important in life and so contribute to the well-being and flourishing of people. We need to distinguish between individual, social and collective hopes. Individual hopes are, for example, one's own health, the acquisition of material things or certain personal projects. Social hopes focus on other people, e.g. on our family members and friends. Collective hopes, on the other hand, relate to political, social, economic and ecological areas of life and are shared by a group of people (Webb, 2013).

The formulation and pursuit of our hopes should be considered with great care, and the desirability of certain values and goals should be assessed consciously. What do I really wish for? What do various other people hope for? In order to understand the paramount social hopes of people in general, we first need to know the personal wishes and hopes of individuals. What people hope for themselves depends on the one hand on individual ideals, ideas and values, and on the other hand on the economic, political and sociocultural conditions of our time.

15.2 Personal Hopes

Just as in the previous ten years, in November 2020, that is during one of the peaks of the worldwide COVID-19 pandemic, we asked around 10,000 people about their personal wishes and hopes. Personal hopes relate to the areas of life that are particularly important to the individual and that are considered possible and achievable regardless of the subjective expectation and assessment of their realization. Thus, personal hopes consciously or unconsciously reflect the idea of desirable futures and in turn shape them to a large extent. Personal hopes are a concretization in the here and now of higher dreams, yearnings or heart's desires.

The 17 areas of life that are presented to the respondents in the Hope Barometer for evaluation relate to the following six categories, which can be rated on a scale of 0 = "not important" to 3 = "very important":

1. Personal well-being (e.g. personal health, harmony);
2. Social relationships (e.g. happy marriage, family, partnership, good relationships with other people);
3. Success and material goods (e.g. more money, success, performance and career);
4. Pleasure and enjoyment (e.g. more sex, romantic experiences, leisure);
5. Security (e.g. in the personal environment or at the workplace);
6. Altruism (e.g. being able to help other people).

Fig. 15.1 presents the means of the personal hopes of the two groups of countries (Europe and outside Europe). As already mentioned, the results

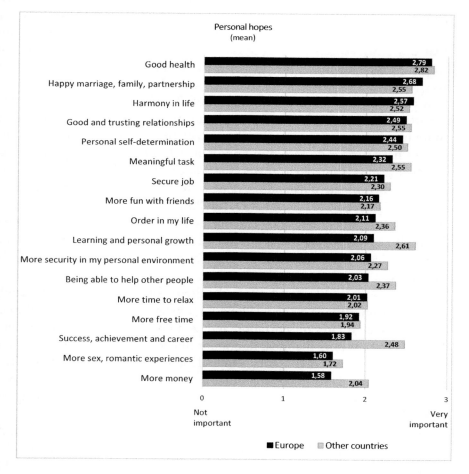

Fig. 15.1 Personal hopes (2020; N=10,230)

are not representative of the societal structure of the countries concerned, but they provide valuable indications with regard to the similarities as well as the varying wishes and hopes of people. An individualized presentation of the results of every single country would go beyond the scope of this book. Here we present the results and findings that allow robust statements after a detailed evaluation and analysis of the statistical data.

There are clear favourites and also areas of unequivocal secondary importance among the most important hopes of people in both groups of countries. It should be noted that the personal hopes were collected in November of the pandemic year 2020. It is surprising how, across all countries, the means of the last ten years almost exactly. Altogether, people in all countries have placed emphasis on the importance of good health, a happy family, marriage or partnership, a harmonious life, good relationships with other people and a meaningful task. These hopes serve personal well-being as well as the strengthening of social relationships and correspond to areas in life that obviously express deep universal values and desires everywhere in the world. At the same time, the categories of money, sex, leisure and relaxation received the lowest rating in all countries studied.

If one compares the hopes at the end of 2020 with the hopes of 2019, it is particularly noticeable that the important things in life have become even more important and that the less important things such as money, sex and success have further decreased in importance. In times of crisis, people focus on what is most valuable to them. The worldwide pandemic has once again clearly shown us the outstanding value of health for our lives. Health is an important prerequisite for an active, fulfilling and happy life. First and foremost, the integrity of our body and our psyche is at stake. At the same time, the health of the population as a whole has a huge impact on almost all areas of our society, which has been painfully recognized during the COVID-19 pandemic.

Another universal hope relates to the desire for a happy marriage, family or partnership. Almost all people long for a loving and stable relationship or family. The high rates of separation and ce do not change this fundamental human need. Among the most important hopes of people are still a harmonious life as well as good and trusting relationships with other people. This highlights the need for inner and outer peace and balance. Most people find daily stress as well as tensions and conflicts to be burdensome, and long for peace, balance and cohesion.

Hope for a meaningful life is a further universal need. It is true for people in both the rich and the poorer countries that the desire for meaningful is usually more important than the desire for a secure job or more money. This was even the case during the pandemic year 2020, even though the hope for a secure job or more money increased in some countries such as India, Israel, Nigeria and Poland. The more uncertain the prospects are in the economy and in the job market, the more important the hope for security becomes. Finally, autonomy, independence and self-determination also belong to a universal hope in that they fulfill the basic human needs to strive for freedom and to make life decisions independently.

In addition to these general similarities, there are also apparent differences between countries. These differences are most clearly visible in six areas that can be divided into two categories. The first category relates to personal and material development. In countries outside Europe, learning and personal growth (in second place in the ranking), personal success in terms of performance and career (in eighth place in the ranking) and more money are significantly more important than for people in Europe. On the one hand, the demographic structure in these countries is younger, which is also reflected in our two groups (the average age in the European sample is around 46 and in the non-European sample around 37). At the same time, the average income (measured by gross domestic product per capita) in countries outside Europe is on average significantly lower than in European countries. It is therefore understandable that young people in poorer, but sometimes ambitious countries such as India, Nigeria, South Africa and Colombia are eager for knowledge, prospects for growth, development opportunities and material well-being. In contrast, these areas are significantly less relevant, although not unimportant, in an aging Europe above all because a large part of the population has already achieved a great deal in these areas.

The second category in which the hopes of people within and outside Europe differ significantly, can be referred to as social cohesion. This includes the areas of order, security and willingness to help others. In countries where economic, political and social conditions make life particularly difficult, people yearn for more stability, security and solidarity between people.

15.3 The Best Possible Self of Young Adults

The personal hopes of people play an important role in shaping desirable future images and personal life plans. Our hopes not only determine what we do, but also who we are (Blöser & Stahl, 2017). As part of a master's course at the University of St. Gallen, the students carried out an exercise in which they worked out images of a desirable future for themselves. The exercise "Best Possible Self" (Sheldon & Lyubomirsky, 2006) was developed in positive psychology and has been tested several times in practice (e.g. Meevissen et al., 2011; Peters et al., 2010). When designing a best possible self, the basic question is how one sees oneself in 20 or 30 years if everything has gone well and one has achieved everything one has wished for. In the course of the exercise, one deals consciously and actively with one's values, interests, dreams and life goals, but at the same time with one's current life situation and activities.

The participants answered the question: "What is the best possible life that I can imagine for myself in the future?" They should deal with as many different areas of life as possible, such as family, job, career, relationships, hobbies and health, and think about what should happen in these areas in the best possible future. Then their ideas about how they might feel in the future, what they would do, what they would have achieved and what was particularly important to them up to that point were recorded.

The exercise was carried out with varying emphases for approximately 15 minutes on five consecutive days. The 13 women and 17 men aged between 22 and 41 (mean 25.4) were able to put themselves into their future selves and write down the spontaneously emerging inner images in detail. It is important that the thoughts about the best possible self do not remain nebulous, but that concrete ideas and possibilities are developed and brought into a logical context. One thinks and visualizes what the best possible self can or should look like if one fully develops one's potential, achieves the most important goals and realizes personal life dreams. In this exercise one concretizes one's future in thoughts, what is particularly important, what one really wants to achieve in life, and considers the outline of one's life as an overall picture.

In this chapter the essential findings from this exercise of the best possible self are presented in general and summarized form. The recurring thought patterns characteristic of the group are discussed and individual comments are cited as a means of illustrating the most important content. In order to protect personal identity, the quotations are published anonymously and with the express consent of the people involved.

In the future images of most of the participants, the private life area took up significantly more space than professional aspects. The focus was clearly on their private lives, and their careers was mentioned relatively rarely. There were fewer pictures about their future jobs than about how they wanted to feel in the future and what was most important to them. For most students, quality of life, well-being, and a fulfilling and satisfying occupation that brings joy and has meaning were much more important than monetary compensation. The job was mentioned as a means to well-being and happiness. It was realized that as a student, one had mostly dealt with career questions and had so far neglected other essential areas in life.

> "When I looked through the diary, I realized that the main topics my texts were dealing with could mainly be assigned to the categories appreciation, harmonious relationships, creation of perspectives and expansion of horizons."

A key finding was that the "best possible self" is not for sale. It was often mentioned that one had been very surprised that material success was not mentioned as an aspect of the best possible self. Topics such as a good purpose in life and intangible values were more important than material things. Interestingly enough, money played an entirely subordinate role for most people.

> "During the exercise, I mainly dealt with the intangible values of my best possible self. The material properties of my future best possible self remained rather in the background during the reflection."

At the beginning of their recordings, some focused on their professional activity and career. They explicitly distinguished between the medium-term and the long-term future. In the following 5 to 10 years, some were fully committed to their careers and saw them as signs of professional success and progress. After graduation, they wanted to prove to themselves and others that they could make something of themselves. The psychological motif behind this is called accomplishment or achievement in psychology. People strive for challenges, want to be successful, achieve goals that are important for them, and experience themselves as competent and effective.

For many, however, more important than the usual themes of power and career are a harmonious coexistence and a respectful interaction between colleagues. Young people want to work in companies where social values have a high priority and the focus is not solely on performance. A responsible task that becomes a calling, in which one can use one's creative abilities and learn something new every day, is a fulfilling one.

> "A calling that gives you the feeling of living right, a meaningful activity for society, a job that does not give you the impression of being stuck in a hamster wheel."

15 to 20 years later, the future looks quite different. The job should become a vocation, but at the same time not lead to one-sidedness and to the detriment of social relationships and hobbies. The theme of work-life balance

was suddenly in the foreground for everyone. One's work should be in harmony with one's mental and physical resources. Satisfaction arises when the "Ich" is in inner balance. Many became aware that they did not want to put career goals above family and social needs. Many (including men) imagined a shorter working time than usual so that they would have enough time for family, child-rearing, friends and other activities.

> "The work-life balance. This often took up a large part in my reports because I am most afraid that I will wake up one day in 15 years and realize that I have neglected my family and "missed" seeing my children grow up due to work."

For many young people, their physical, mental, emotional and social health was in the foreground. This includeds conscious nutrition, the consumption of sustainable products, sport and physical exercise, their relation to the natural and social environment, and the maintenance of fulfilling relationships.

> "For me, a recurrent theme was relaxation. 'I feel relaxed and balanced' or 'I feel as if I have arrived somewhere' are sentences that I take from my notes."

The need for fulfilling, harmonious and stable social relationships and for good physical and mental health was expressed time and again. Particularly characteristic of the best possible self are appreciative relationships with oneself, with other people and with the environment as a whole. Good relationships between partners, with children, with family members, friends, colleagues and superiors. Mutual trust and support, as well as talking to and maintaining contact with one another are all part of a good relationship.

> "I have noticed in particular that the central leitmotif of connectedness to other people has come up again and again and that the ideas regarding family and relationship were much clearer than the ideas in the other areas, and the associated feelings have given me much more."

A recurring theme is the desire for inner and outer harmony. Harmony between the areas family, work and hobbies as well as in relationships with other people and with the environment. A harmonious coexistence is characterized by mutual acceptance, support and caring as well as by trust, mindfulness and availability.

> "Harmony is the central instance of my best possible self. A harmonious state of family, career, mind and body."

It was often recognized that happiness in life is hardly achieved by material possessions alone. Values such as integrity, friendliness, cordiality, understanding, helpfulness, gratitude, and awareness of sustainability were mentioned frequently. One's own happiness can be achieved above all by increasing the satisfaction and quality of life of one's fellow human beings. Furthermore, one felt the need to change certain things in society. By helping others, one increases one's own joie de vivre and quality of life.

> "My best possible self was less about material wishes. Rather, it was about interpersonal relationships, deep and fruitful conversations, social engagement, (spiritual) personal development and realization, as well as an idyllic, independent and harmonious life in accord with nature."

At the end of this chapter, we would like to expand these self-portraits of young academics through the representative results of the Generation Barometer, which was carried out extensively in Switzerland (Bühler, 2020). The Generation Barometer has surveyed and analyzed the dreams and expectations of various age groups in Switzerland.

In past centuries it was believed that each new generation would have a better life than the previous one. Young adults today no longer see it that way. Most 18- to 24-year-olds believe that their parents had it better than they themselves do. Due to the increasing pressure to succeed and perform, less attractive job prospects and the poorer state of nature, young adults no longer believe in further progress in terms of their own quality of life. Despite the general prosperity and current satisfaction in life, there is a pronounced deficit of hope in this age group. A majority of young adults suffer from general disillusionment and hopelessness with regard to the future.

It seems that young adults are missing something in their lives, for example more peace and relaxation, a fulfilling partnership and confidence in the future. It is striking that none of the four most mentioned dreams of young adults are material things. In addition to the dream of a great trip and a good partnership, the younger generation wishes for more meaningful activities through which they can do some good for others. Many young people wish for more solidarity and greater social commitment. In view of their great importance, we will examine the social and societal dimensions of hope in the following chapters and explain the conditions for them.

16

The Social Dimension of Hope

Hope is an eminently social phenomenon. We hope most strongly when we feel connected to other people, when we hope for and with others and when we feel carried and supported by others. Loneliness, on the other hand, is the greatest enemy of hope. People who feel abandoned in their hopes, not taken seriously or even rejected, report significantly lower hope values and suffer from anxiety and depression to a greater extent. Hope thrives in the feeling of security, trust and belonging to a group of like-minded people that is characterized by appreciation, compassion, solidarity and mutual helpfulness. Our ability to hope is not only strengthened by the care and support of others. It also thrives through our own willingness to hope for others and to give them courage and self-confidence in difficult times. By standing by other people when they need us, we inspire our own hope as well as that of others.

16.1 Social Support

An important finding of psychology and philosophy is the social character of hope (Erikson, 1998; Marcel, 1949; McGeer, 2008). Hope is not just a private mental state. The activity of hoping thrives in the interplay between the person and their social and natural environment. The social character of hope was most prominently highlighted by the philosopher Gabriel Marcel (1949). Gabriel Marcel emphasizes a hope that is directed towards a community of two people. For Marcel, hope is fundamentally relationship-oriented, i.e. a practice of life that is based on relationships. For Marcel, hope is that quality through which we are able to look beyond ourselves and our limits and which directs our attention to what is possible with the help of

© The Author(s), under exclusive license to Springer-Verlag GmbH, DE, part of Springer Nature 2022
A. M. Krafft, *Our Hopes, Our Future*, https://doi.org/10.1007/978-3-662-66205-2_16

others. In hope, the focus is not only placed on an object, but above all on another person with and for whom we hope.

Thus hope arises through the bond of love and through attention to another person. Only this personal relationship based on love makes the emergence of a robust hope possible, one that is even unconditional. When we hope unconditionally, we hope not only for and by ourselves, but for, and together with someone else as well. This shared hope gives people a special strength to overcome feelings of helplessness and hopelessness. Social hope is especially important in the case of illness and other adversities in life. Hope is drawn from the relationship to another person; it defies adverse situations in life and grows beyond them. In contrast, destructive relationships as well as the feelings of loneliness and social rejection are amplifiers of helplessness and hopelessness, and therefore of anxiety and worry, during difficult life phases.

In the Hope Barometer from November 2019, we examined social rejection for the first time using the scale developed by Cyranowski et al. (2013) in connection to hope as well as to anxiety and depression (Kroenke et al., 2009). Social rejection occurs when people have the impression that their hopes are not important to others, that others are not interested in them. When this happens, people feel as if they were irrelevant to others. If one were to ask someone for help and support, one would either not be taken seriously or feel abandoned.

Of the approximately 10,000 people surveyed, around 12 to 14% experienced massive social rejection, and around a quarter of the population sometimes felt alone and rejected. The connection this has with hope and the feelings of anxiety and depression can be seen in Fig. 16.1. The higher the social rejection, the lower the perceived hope and the higher the anxiety and depression.

In hoping we can establish a new kind of relationship with others. According to Kadlac (2015), hope is a virtue, especially when it generates empathy and solidarity with others. Good hope is a hope of mutual caring. Since our well-being is closely related to our relationships with other people, hope will be a continuous social activity (Stitzlein, 2019). Our hope is strengthened when we realize that others are concerned about our well-being. This makes us aware of how important and invigorating our mutual attention, encouragement, and support are for maintaining our hopes and those of others.

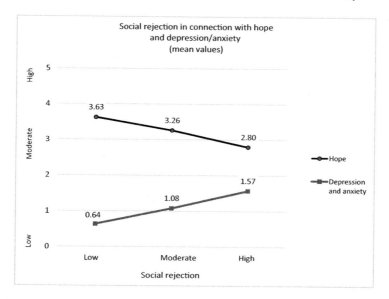

Fig. 16.1 Social rejection in connection with hope as well as depression and anxiety (2019; N = 10,907)

The hope and well-being of the individual depend on the feeling of belonging and trust in oneself and in others, combined with a clear conviction of what life is really about and what is worth hoping for (Braithwaite, 2004). By listening to the views of other people who care about us, we can also question and correct our hopes. We expand our hope through a trusting connection with others. While fear alienates and separates us, hope creates a bond of appreciation and trust, thanks to which we commit ourselves to our hopes but can also realign them if some should fail. From this shared existence arises a community of hope (McGeer, 2004).

16.2 Receiving Support

Hope is fundamentally a social phenomenon. Without the support of other people, our own ability to act and hope would be severely limited. On the one hand, we rely on our abilities and actively develop them in shaping and pursuing our hopes. On the other hand, we have to accept our limits and seek a connection to other people who practically and emotionally support us in realizing our hopes.

The social value of hope can be seen basically on three levels. First, we sometimes need the active support and assistance of others in order to realize our hopes. Second, other people can hope for and with us. Through emotional support and personal encouragement, we gain self-confidence and feel "empowered". Third, it is about the formation of a community of hope in which people work together and commit themselves to their common values, interests and ideals for and with each other.

In order to achieve our goals, we often have to work with other people, rely on their support and trust them. In interpersonal hope, we expand our own ability to act by placing our hope in other people, whether it be in family members, colleagues, doctors, or the government (Martin, 2019). As we noted in section 10.3, support from family and friends is one of the most important sources of hope. A loving relationship with family and friends plays a particularly important role for all aspects of hope: we are affirmed in our wishes, can believe in ourselves and in new possibilities, and trust in active support when we need it.

The results in Fig. 16.2 (measured with the questionnaire by Cyranowski et al., 2013) show how pronounced social support is in society. More than half of our survey participants had someone who listened to them when they

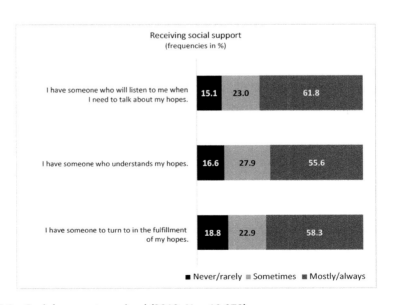

Fig. 16.2   Social support received (2019; N = 10,970)

wanted to talk about their hopes, who understood their hopes, and to whom they could turn in fulfilling their hopes. For about a quarter of the respondents this was sometimes, but not usually, the case. In contrast, between 15 and 20% rarely or never felt supported by someone else.

The social dimension of hope is particularly important when we have to struggle with difficulties and disappointments. Especially in difficult times we need the availability and supportive affection of other people who believe in and with us, especially when we can no longer do things on our own. We know then that we are not alone and that, should we ever not know the next step, others will be there to give us courage and hope. In view of daily tasks and hurdles, this certainty protects us from impending helplessness and despair. Through the gift of hope, we are both the shapers of our lives and the grateful recipients of the caring affection of others. In this way we connect strength and humility, eagerness for action and patience, giving and taking.

When others hope for us and on our behalf, they see us as we could be. They convey to us respect and appreciation. They believe in us even when we no longer believe in ourselves and thereby generate new self-confidence in us (McGeer, 2008). Others reinforce our hopes through their encouragement, their presence and their active support. When other people are there for us, believe in us, encourage us and advocate for us, this strengthens our hope, our faith and our willpower. Once this is reciprocal, we will empower ourselves through our hope and at the same time also encourage others (McGeer, 2004).

The almost linear relationship between these two phenomena is shown in Fig. 16.3.

Thanks to the encouragement of other people, we feel reassured, take our strengths more self-confidently into account, and develop a positive and hopeful attitude towards the future. By placing their trust in us, others strengthen and enable us to do and be what we can. When others show hopeful trust in us, we ourselves can hope more firmly. The appreciation that others indicate through their faith and trust in us revives our general ability to hope and trust in our own desires and strengths. We see our future as something that we can shape through our own ability to act and with the support of others. Therefore, we should always seek out people who are able to confirm our hopes and at the same time are willing to support others in realizing their hopes.

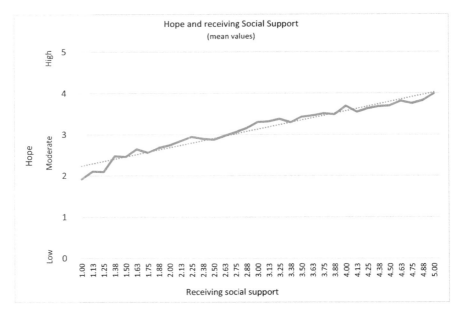

Fig. 16.3 Receiving hope in relation to social support (2019; N = 10,970)

16.3 Giving Support

Sometimes people give us hope. In other situations, we are the ones who can give hope to others. Hope is a gift with which we enable people and thereby also enable ourselves, such as when parents hope for their children (McGeer, 2004, 2008). By supporting other people in their willingness and ability to hope, we show them our trust in their hopes. We thereby convey to them the feeling that their wishes and hopes are important to us and so offer them our respect and recognition. Just by caring about and being interested in the hopes of others, we signalize how valuable their hopes are, which lends their hopes new energy. By believing in others, we confirm their own belief in the feasibility of their wishes and encourage them to stand fast and not give up. People can thereby develop a hopeful energy that can infect others and in turn confirm their hopes.

Marcel's (1949) concept of "availability" is central to the understanding of hope. Often the best way to help another person is simply to be there, to listen to them and to establish an emotional connection. In hoping, we are open and available to others. They can trust us and count on our attention and support. This acknowledges the mutual dependence we have on each other. When we open ourselves up and make ourselves available to someone, we do so in the belief in that person. This leads to a creative relationship and a shared commitment to a cause. We become carriers of hope for our environment by upholding common ideals, believing in a good future for all, trusting in the abilities of others and supporting them in the realization of their hopes.

The importance of the need to be there for others, to listen to them and to convey a sense of security is evident in Fig. 16.4.

Hope lives in concrete relationships, especially in the ideals and values we share with family and friends. People who maintain good relationships with their partners, family members and friends feel more hopeful. In addition, a happy marriage, family or partnership, as well as positive and trusting human relationships, are among the most important personal hopes of most people (see Section 15.2.). One's partner and family are both essential sources and important goals of hope. Especially relevant is the experience of mutual helpfulness and support, i.e. being there for each other when the partner and family need it. Hope is linked to selflessness here. Just talking to one's spouse or partner can already be understood as one of the most important foundations of hope.

The significant relationship between one's own hope and the willingness to be there and support others is evident in Fig. 16.5. The more we listen

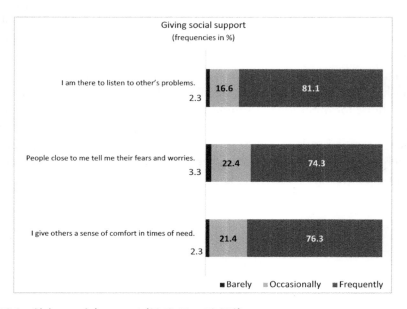

Fig. 16.4 Giving social support (2019; N = 10,970)

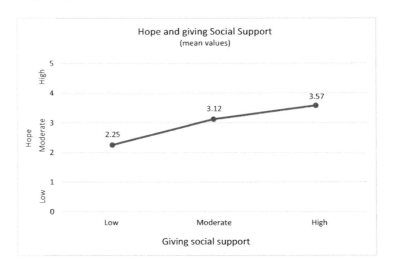

Fig. 16.5 Hope in relation to social support given (2019; N = 10,970)

to others, encourage them and give them a feeling of trust and security, the stronger our own hope.

All of this points to the importance of mutual caring and helpfulness in preserving hope. The consistent conclusion of these phenomena is that our ability and willingness to hope depend on how well we can hope not only for ourselves, but also with and for others, thus forming a community of hope (McGeer, 2004). Once we respond to the hopes of others, we take part in their lives and open up our own horizon for hope. We need to take care of both ourselves and others, which in turn emphasizes the essential role of family, friends and community as carriers of hope (Snow, 2019). When we share our hopes with other people, we hope in solidarity. Sometimes we only hope for others out of simple attentiveness. But if we are interested and committed to the well-being of others, e.g. for our partner, children etc., then we hope for them out of love. In this way, a network of hopeful people emerges who are there for each other and help each other. People with common goals develop a collective hope in this way (Martin, 2019).

17

Societal Hope

Social progress, as history of humanity shows us, is driven by shared visions of a better world and the pragmatic hope for individual and collective agency in shaping the future. On the one hand, we need clear ideas about how society should develop. Instead of dystopian images of a collapsing earth, we need more realistic utopias of a flourishing world. To avoid falling into despair and helplessness, these utopias must be linked to the pragmatic idea that together we can shape the world we want. Communities of collective hope are held together by shared images of a desirable future and by the belief in the feasibility of these wishes. Such communities of hope can be found, for example, in non-profit and volunteer organizations and clubs that have the common good as their goal and live from the commitment, mutual support and trust of their members.

17.1 Pragmatic Hope

Philosophical pragmatism and meliorism assume that the world is not perfect, but also that the future is not predetermined so that together we can make it better. Pragmatists direct their hope towards what can be done and improved in the present for the future. A belief in goodness in life, as Dewey (1916/1980) argues, is a prerequisite for serious commitment to a better world. While a society dominated by fear will be characterized by egoism and competition, a community of hope will lead to greater cohesion, solidarity and mutual cooperation (Stahl, 2019).

Meliorism à la Dewey includes the belief that we cannot foresee the future, but that the conditions that exist at any particular moment, be they

© The Author(s), under exclusive license to Springer-Verlag GmbH, DE, part of Springer Nature 2022
A. M. Krafft, *Our Hopes, Our Future*, https://doi.org/10.1007/978-3-662-66205-2_17

bad or good, can always be improved. Meliorism is defined as "the idea that at least there is a sufficient basis of goodness in life and its conditions so that by thought and earnest effort we may constantly make things better." (Dewey, 1916/1980, p. 294). This includes a belief in the possibilities that the future offers us and a joint willingness to seize these possibilities. Neither living conditions nor our efforts are assumed to be given and unchangeable.

In difficult times we can improve our lives and the lives of others and overcome despair or discouragement. Dewey's understanding of hope as a social force consists in the ability to believe that our shared future will simply be different, freer and better than the past. Even if we do not know exactly how the world will look in ten, twenty or thirty years and we cannot form a precise image of the future, we can believe that if we work together, we can create a better world regardless of how bad the situation may seem at the moment (Rorty, 1999). However, we need to trust that we are not the only ones who want to improve the world.

In order to change something together, we need concrete ideals. These ideals serve to expand our horizon and perspectives and must therefore be developed and maintained in concert. The more conscious these ideals are, the more they can motivate us to act and cooperate. For Rorty (1999), social progress, in which we should set our hopes, consists of an increasingly sensitive awareness of the needs of an ever greater variety of people. The ideal of social democracy considers all people to be equal, treats them with equal respect and sees them as jointly partaking in a common life. The hope for a world in which there can be more justice and less suffering is directed at concrete concerns such as that every human being has enough to eat, a worthy home, and access to medical care and education (Rorty, 2002).

According to Rorty, the value of hope lies in the belief that the future can be designed better than the past. Hope lives in an undefined utopia, in a belief that there are different ways to realize it, and in trust in the powers of collective action. Hope means for Rorty (1998, p. 138), "taking the world by the throat and insisting that there is more to this life than we have ever imagined."

Shared hope for a better world promotes cooperation between people. Through shared experiences, values and interests, a sense of mutual solidarity and common hope can develop. Social hope is a series of positive habits that create new possibilities and through close cooperation with others make the world a better place.

17.2 Collective Hope

Collective hope is a special form of social hope, namely the shared wishes and visions of a meaningful and dignified life within a social community (Kleist & Jansen, 2016). A community is a society or group of people held together and guided by shared interests and values (Stahl, 2019). Collective hope refers to the hope that people have together with others for the implementation of certain values and dreams of a community. We speak of a collective hope when a whole group of people has shared convictions and wishes and brings them to fruition in a hopeful way (Blöser & Stahl, 2019).

In a community of hopes, the conditions are first created on the basis of which the shared hopes can take shape. A key question is therefore what we together can hope for and what hopes we should have in each other. A clarification of the value and meaning of the desired hopes takes place. The collective process of hope begins with a desirecd vision of social change and seizing opportunities for its implementation (Braithwaite, 2004a).

What holds societies together are shared hopes of a better collective future (Rorty, 2002). This type of hope connects us with other people with whom we can build a global network of social hope. Instead of just focusing on our individual goals, we let ourselves be involved in a larger community with higher social, ecological or even material goals and pursue them together. The focus is on how we can learn and change individually and thus also improve the world around us.

Hope for social change such as for more justice brings people together by giving them a sense of a shared mission. A shared vision of the future and hope for a better life connect us with other people, promote the common good, and give people a sense of meaning in life (Stitzlein, 2019). In such a community of hope, people are psychologically and practically united through the shared hopes.

A community of hope requires shared values and ideals, but also a shared commitment. In this way, the members of the community work for the realization of the shared goals. Communities are especially important for overcoming obstacles and difficulties, which can lead to a unifying identity. In social hope, we recognize the difficulties of the current situation and at the same time believe that things can be improved by us and others. The conditions for joint action are created in the community, and when difficulties arise, the belief and trust in the realization of the hopes are strengthened.

One could consider a society to be flourishing if it makes progress in the realization of its shared social vision (McGeer, 2004).

True communities are characterized by a genuine concern for their members. A community of hope is characterized by procedures of mutual support. It constitutes a unit and an identity, thanks to which it promotes positive interpersonal relationships. In a community not only the common cause is involved, but also the respect and ability of each individual member. A community of hope consists in people sharing their ideals and values, believing in goodness, trusting in their various abilities and supporting each other. Such a community is characterized by a spirit of care and cohesion instead of by one of egoism, suspicion and worry (McGeer, 2004).

It is important that every person feel connected to a particular community, as this empowers and encourages them. They can get involved and make a contribution that they otherwise would not have been able to make. By belonging to a social community, one's effectiveness and self-esteem are strengthened. With the empowering force of a community we can expand our individual ability to act and hope. What we cannot achieve alone can be realized throughcooperation within a community as a result of the individual contributions of all the members. To the extent that shared goals and a sense of empowerment shape the group identity and the individual's sense of belonging, cooperation within the group is strengthened (Braithwaite, 2004a). A community is then viable when its members can make their individual contributions, express and develop their personality, and be appreciated and supported by others (Shade, 2019).

It is most valuable is when a community of hope can promote a hopeful future perspective independently of concrete hopes. This nourishes the hope above and beyond the individual hopes that a community will maintain even when particular goals cannot be achieved or changed for the time being. Webb (2013) speaks of a transformative hope in which the future is not seen as predetermined but can be actively shaped by people. Hope is transformative because it critically accepts the current situation and is driven by the desire for a better future. It promotes the development of new possibilities and the shared trust in one's ability to realize them. Its basic message is: we can take the problems of humanity into our own hands and together change things.

17.3 Hope and Realistic Utopias

The utopian thinking anchored in future research is associated with hope for a better future and the resulting critical engagement with current social conditions and trends. Ernst Bloch (1959) directly linked the concept of utopia with the phenomenon of hope. The value of utopias lies in the explicit engagement with current conditions and the design of completely new and to some extent "unrealistic" future images. Current problems are to be overcome mentally and the ideal state of a perfect society is to be visualized.

It was Frank Polak (1973) who, with his work "The Image of the Future", highlighted the great importance of utopias in the context of the social and cultural development of countries and thus decisively shaped social science future research. In his opinion, utopian thinking about the future has contributed significantly to the progress of general thinking and awareness. The task of the utopia is to hold up two mirrors to people: one that reflects the current situation and one that reflects an image of a possible and better future. Consciousness of the problems and difficulties that one would like to overcome in the hope of molding history evolves when a utopia begins to develop. The task of utopias is the creative development of positive future images. With the idea of a better future, utopias overcome the alleged determinism of anticipated trends and open up the horizon for new possibilities. Utopias serve as drivers of the future and as triggers for social progress.

Concrete utopias historically show themselves in latent trends. They are historically present as an element of culture, and they point forward towards the emerging future. Realistic utopias are located within reality and relate to what Bloch (1949) calls the Front and the Novum. Realistic utopias show the direction for progress in this world. They exceed current reality and announce a new reality. What Bloch described in the social realm is called the "leading edge" in science and research today : the most advanced position in a certain area. These are namely the developments that go beyond the current "state of the art" and bring something partially or completely new to light. The current reality is thereby transcended, i.e. transformed and surpassed.

Utopias have repeatedly called into question and changed prevailing world and human images and thus brought about a major turning point in history. History always shows how long new ideas need to mature before they can become the common property of a people. Many utopian ideas that arise in the imagination find their way into social reality decades later. No social achievements would exist if the principles of their design had not been conceived as an idea long before and if this ideal had not motivated people to action. Inasmuch as it is an intellectual experiment, the utopia is the spiritual father of modern society.

Due to the failed experiments of socialist utopias, today one hardly speaks anymore of utopias, but rather of visions of a desirable and sustainable world (Costanza & Kubiszewski, 2014). Concrete ideas such as human rights, equality, environmental protection, social institutions, humanitarian aid, etc. found their forerunners among social visionaries. Visionaries are those people who have an idea long before it has become common property of society. Utopian visions are the forerunners of all modern ideas about social policy, social organizations and peace. Today's generally accepted concept of social security took shape centuries ago in utopian future images that were once considered merely the fantasies of utopian thinkers. Such was also the case of parliamentary democracy, universal suffrage and the representation of the interests of workers by a trade union. A utopia led the emancipation of women long before the formation of the women's movement. All of today's concepts of work, from the length of the working week to the participation in profits, originated in a utopia. Utopias have always been powerful levers of social progress. Practically everything that man considers different and better in the social field in the last centuries was originally part of or the result of utopian visions.

For Rorty (2002), we have to dream the future. With utopian future images one would like to hold on to dreams of a better world and to inspire a greater number of people support their realization. Our belief in the possibilities of the dreamt goal does not lie in evidence, but in the inspiring quality of the goal itself. One would like to make the seemingly impossible possible through the power of the hope and conviction with which the novelty has been dreamt and . For Gutierrez (2001), hope sets us free. Visions and utopias offer people the image of an ideal future to which one can commit oneself, and emphasize human freedom and dignity. Man is always free to imagine a completely different and better world and to strive for it. In utopian hope, the world is experienced as open for communal design.

A utopia, according to Ernst Bloch, is an expression of hope, not only as a feeling, but essentially as a guiding idea for active shaping of the world. From the perspective of the realistic utopia, pure wishful thinking lacks the will to effect change (see sect. 13.2.). The world is essentially unfinished, and concrete utopias are all the more important because they represent a possible future that lies within reality. The utopian image should span the horizon of real possibilities and convey the feeling that the future can be different from the present and that the desired state is both striving for and achievable (Webb, 2013).

The utopia grasps at a better future and thus anticipates it. It involves not only a dream, but also the will to realize it. For Bloch, the concrete and hopeful utopia anticipates and shapes the future at the same time. Only this strong-willed utopia involves hope. Bloch describes an abstract utopia as immature fantasy and daydreaming that are not oriented toward real possibilities. With hope, utopian wishful thinking is transformed into a strong-willed and effective action. Hopeful utopias include not only the idea of what might be possible in the future, but also the means and ways to achieve it.

17.4 Need for Utopian Visions of the Future

In view of undesirable realities and future images, a new need for utopian visions of the future arises in many areas today. Alternative ideas and models have been designed and means of implementation proposed that would allow them to develop into common utopias. A variety of alternative concepts have been developed for schools, business and other areas of life; these are referred to as "the school of the future" (Heinrich et al., 2020), "the economy of the future" (Felder, 2018), "agriculture of the future" (Gruber, 2009) or in general "the world of the future". They are dreams of a better life that naturally go beyond the present reality and extend into a changed future.

At the beginning of the twenty-first century, however, these or similar utopias had not yet reached the general awareness of the population. Just as Habermas (1985) diagnosed an "exhaustion of utopian energies", Gordin et al. (2010) stated that we would live in a post-utopian society today. In the twentieth and twenty-first centuries, great social visions have become rather rare. The lack of belief in a social utopia, i.e. a better world, has led to a pessimistic attitude about the future in many people.

Current studies show impressively that many people (especially young people) have more dystopian (negative) than utopian future images today (Gordin et al., 2010; Nordensward, 2014). On the one hand, we have achieved a great deal in modern society. Many dreams and utopias of the past have come true. We live longer, travel farther and are doing better than ever before. But the social ability to develop new and different future images has declined sharply in the last 50 years (Slaughter, 1994). In many areas there is a lack of positive models for the future that could provide orientation and direction as well as trust and belief that the current problems of the world can be solved.

For Fred Polak (1973), future images are like mirrors of their respective zeitgeist. The degree of hope or hopelessness is a measure of the health and well-being of the population. The lack of positive utopian ideas is a hindrance to social progress, especially because the future becomes a projection field of fears instead of hopes. According to Polak, one needs to ask whether the decline of utopian thinking is not synonymous with a decline of social progress itself. He is convinced that the lack of acceptance of utopian future images is a sign of the powerlessness and the lost belief in the self-determination of man in our time. While in past centuries old world views were replaced by new future ideals, unique about our present time is the absence of utopian future images.

According to Webb (2008), the framework in which utopian thoughts can arise at all must be recreated in our time. The value of utopian thinking therefore does not depend on whether "better" future visions are , but rather on the promotion of utopian and transformative ideas.

17.5 Institutions of Hope

In institutions of hope such as schools, communities, clubs, etc., people can learn to believe in the future and actively commit themselves to the extraordinary (Braithwaite, 2004). We already have valuable communities of hope that manifest themselves in voluntary and charitable work in communities and clubs. In a representative survey of the Swiss Generations Barometer (Bühler et al., 2020), the need for a meaningful activity or task was the most frequently mentioned longing of all. Many people have the desire to engage in voluntary work in order to do good to others. A large majority of the population across all political parties in Switzerland even supports the introduction of mandatory community service for everyone.

Voluntary organizations (aid associations, clubs, churches, etc.) are lively communities of hope in which one's own actions are connected to those of others. Grassroots initiatives for more environmental protection, justice, development aid and many other such areas reflect a yearning for change to a better future. Such institutions of hope kindle a baseline mood that certain goals are worth striving for and generate a belief in their realization (Braithwaite, 2004b; Green, 2008).

Institutions of hope make people active and responsible creators of a vibrant civil society. Aid organizations are a testimony to the moving power of hope in that through their commitment they promote the ideals of help-fulness, community spirit and growth. Volunteer work means active com-mitment to hopes whose realization does not only or immediately concern just ourselves. We can help and inspire others to commit themselves to a better future. Through voluntary commitment, we invest our time in the lives of others and beyond our personal hopes. Service to others is an evident expression of hope and faith. It awakens a belief in a better future and pro-motes commitment to it. On the one hand, such institutions awaken hope in a valuable goal or ideal, and on the other hand, they empower us to act.

18

The Desirable World of Young Adults

Designing the best possible world begins with a mental journey into the future in which personal imagination is used to overcome current obstacles and problems. In thought, one designs different worlds out of life such as work, family, environment, education, social relationships, etc., as they should look in 20–30 years according to one's values and ideals. Young university students openly gave information about their future fears and concerns and sketched a best possible world for themselves in which they wanted to live, work and raise their children. They gave information about what is particularly important to them, how social and technological progress should take place in their eyes, and how people should live together and relate to the environment. Actively sketching a best possible world lets people draw various registers: mental visions are accompanied by a cocktail of emotions as well as self-reflection, fundamental questions and an energetic will to act.

18.1 The Best Possible World

Social science future research combines the individual needs of people with social and ecological habitats, whereby the general quality of life receives the main focus. Future research has recognized very early on that it makes little sense to focus only on problems. What really sustains us are hopes and dreams in the form of positive visions and future designs of a more livable and sustainable world. It is human hopes that release the energy for a better future.

The second exercise with the master's students at the University of St. Gallen related to the imagination and conceptualization of a best possible world. In this exercise, which has its origins in social science future research

© The Author(s), under exclusive license to Springer-Verlag GmbH, DE, part of Springer Nature 2022
A. M. Krafft, *Our Hopes, Our Future*, https://doi.org/10.1007/978-3-662-66205-2_18

(Boulding, 1994; Eckersley, 1999; Hicks, 1994; Jungk & Müllert, 1989), the focus is not on one's own life, but on the quality of life in general and on relevant social and ecological environments. If one assumes that not only one's own future, but also the future of mankind is designable, then the first question should be what kind of future is desirable anyway. In other words, this is about visions of a better world. This, in turn, requires a normative assessment, i.e. an assessment of what is right and what is wrong, what is good and what is bad, not only for the individual, but also for the families and communities in which we live, as well as for society and the planet as a whole. Important, as the word "best possible" already implies, is that a future vision is seen as both desirable and possible.

In this exercise the participants set out on a mental journey into the future (in 20–30 years). The creative value of the exercise lies in overcoming current reality and developing completely new ideas and wishes. By thinking about the world in which they would like to live, people can let their imagination and dreams run free. They are asked to include details in order to be able to see clearly what this world looks like. What are the most important properties and characteristics of their best possible future? What areas are affected (environment, work, economy, politics, health, family, social relationships, education, schools, universities, etc.)? What do people, children, older people, men, women, etc. do? How do the cities look? Ultimately, all of these questions are about creating a livable world in which not only economic prosperity, but also the individual and social well-being of as many people as possible and in addition the natural environment play an essential role.

Developing desirable future scenarios is usually not a purely cognitive and rational exercise. When it comes to planning alternative future designs, creativity and intuition, and thus emotions, values, hopes, fears, dreams and yearnings become increasingly significant. These phenomena can be recorded as creatively as possible by using various elements such as colorful images, drawings, collages and texts.

18.2 Future and Fears and Concerns of Young Adults

Before they turned to their desirable future visions, many participants reflected on their concerns and fears. Against the background of the current world situation, the prospects of the future appear desolate and frightening to many young people. Humanity is facing enormous challenges such as climate change, poverty alleviation and the solution of international conflicts. The students recognized the causes in the selfishness and greed of ruthless capitalism, in the ignorance and disrespect of many people and in the dominant anthropocentric world view. The dominance of the Western (rich) countries over the developing countries was seen as an obstacle explains why goods and food that are actually available in abundance do not reach the needy.

Young adults view the current political and economic development of Europe with concern. The declining cohesion between the European countries, above all the withdrawal of Great Britain from the EU, the growth of right-wing parties and the EU-hostile slogans of some politicians represent a danger to stability, tolerance and peace.

Their doubt about the possibility of positive development lies for some in the bogged down state of the current social structure. One is stuck fast politically and socially and can see no progress whatsoever in recent years. In accordance with the results presented in chapters four and five, many young people fear a deterioration of the current global problems. Many are concerned about the environment, the economy and the unemployment, and consciously or unconsciously have various fears: on the one hand fear of the destruction of the environment and thus of our lebensraum, on the other hand fear of being overwhelmed and failing personally. Simultaneously many feel powerless because they have the impression that they can do little about the situation.

Paradoxically, doubt about today's society prevents the evolution of thoughts about a better future, as if the image of a failing society were anchored in one's consciousness. As a result of the perceived hopelessness, some young adults do not want to have children. Others are more confident that humanity will be able to solve the current problems. In particular experiences during the Corona crisis have revealed the solidarity and helpfulness of people towards one another, but also their fears.

18.3 The Best Possible World of Young Adults

All participants in the exercise agreed that the best possible future should not be dominated by power struggles, greed for money, or by material possessions. Among the ideas for a best possible world, the topics environment and social affairs were at the forefront. Almost all students focused on as green and social world as the main emphasis of their desirable future. Images of a desirable world dealt with the rectification of current problems such as climate change, environmental pollution, social injustice, racism and current working conditions. The most frequently mentioned topics were sustainability, cohesion, peace, harmony, justice, freedom, well-being and joy. Violence and oppression have no place in this world. Above all, young people are concerned with natural, human and in part spiritual aspects of life.

> "Through the exercise I realized that the perfect world does not need much luxury or diverse science fiction technologies to be perfect. What counts in my best possible world is that all people are treated equally and fairly, stand together and are simply happy."
>
> "The longer I did the exercise, the more vivid the images became in my head. My best possible world is green and colorful, sustainable and liberal, social and 'slowed down'."

Recurring motifs of a desirable future were an environmentally friendly economy (e.g. CO_2-neutral), the use of sustainable energy sources and the renunciation of fossil fuels. There should be more nature and wilderness in the world in the future. More responsible and above all reduced consumption would attest to respect for the earth. There was a desire for conscious consumption of health-promoting and environmentally friendly products. People would only consume what they absolutely needed and pay attention to the environment when buying goods. Information about products would increasingly disclose the origin and production conditions, for example, so that customers, company employees and the public are informed of the products' ethical and moral backgrounds. In this way consumption and commitment to the company could be evaluated with regard to sustainability and morality.

In a desirable world, environmental protection and sustainability should be given a prominent place at all levels of education. Through education, the connections between our actions and the environment become understandable. Topics such as sustainability and respect for other living things should be cultivated starting in kindergarten, throughout the school years and including all levels of adult education.

> "If I close my eyes and imagine a beautiful world, then I see nature, for example green meadows, crystal-clear lakes, paradise beaches and a bright blue sky. What I definitely don't see are big cities, production facilities or highways. All my ideas of the best possible world were free of material values and consumption. In addition to the environment, these scenarios are about happy and satisfied people who have enough time to enjoy their lives and their families in addition to their work."

"The image of the best possible world in general was mostly green for me. Buildings whose roofs flow into the landscape next to treetops and bodies of water that transport clear and clean water."

The possibilities and effects of technological progress were assessed partly positively and optimistically, partly critically or at least ambivalently. Innovative thinking would find environmentally friendly solutions in the future. Technological developments should relieve the environment and strengthen community between people (e.g. through digital communication tools). Environmentally friendly vehicles and factories as well as sustainable energy sources could conserve the planet's limited resources, reduce environmental pollution and thus overcome the climate crisis.

"It is important to me that scientific research should not contribute to greater economic success, but to a better life for people."

Technological progress could strengthen the economy and reduce unemployment together with the associated social conflicts. In addition, new technologies could close the gap between rich and poor by creating healthy and sustainable jobs. The Internet, for example, could reduce the knowledge gap between countries. Through the Internet children in poorer countries could be taught better and receive a high-quality education. In their visions of the future, some students also hoped that medical and technological progress would lead to the cure of chronic and incurable diseases. This hope is an expression of humanity and compassion and is driven by a deep desire to free affected people and their families from suffering.

"Thanks to advances in medicine, people are physically and mentally fit far into old age. Due to automation and technical progress, prosperity does not increase at the expense of sustainability. People focus again on the essentials and increasingly seek physical relationships instead of social media and are more connected to nature."

Our current economic system has brought with it numerous negative consequences, including an overexertion and overburdening of people through enormous pressure at work. The psychological and physical damage caused by excessive work orientation is immense. New technologies such as digitalization could provide novel tools and work models in the future and enable a more harmonious balance between work performance and personal health. If a better balance between economic output and work mode were made possible, the current work overload and the health problems caused by it could be remedied. The idea of a decelerated world with a stronger focus on community was mentioned frequently. Mechanical and repetitive work such as operating a till or stocking shelves could be taken over by robots so that people could focus on meaningful tasks for society and the environment.

> "In my ideal future, I saw green spaces in cities again and again and people moving in them. They look much more balanced than today. Furthermore, the world of work has changed, from a capitalist-driven always-more-work world to a work world in which people can live without the pressure that they can't do enough or are too unproductive."

On the other hand, technological progress was compared with progress in human consciousness. A one-sided focus on would not serve human beings if they did not see to a balanced diet, sustainable economic activity, harmonious relationships with other human beings and their physical, emotional and mental health in a more conscious way. The main question is not how to develop even better and more efficient technologies, but how can the human being develop physically, mentally and socially into a better human being and contribute on the whole to making a better world.

Therefore, we should worry less about new technologies and material goods than about ourselves, our health, our human values, and other people who we can look after. Progress is not achieved through new technologies and competition, but through joint action. The focus is on mutual understanding and respectful treatment of one another as the basis for harmony, security and trust.

> "Furthermore, humanity has understood its dependence on nature, but also on each other, and has freed itself from a fast and superficial life. They have realized that they are part of something bigger and thus gain a higher consciousness."

In the desirable future, every person is not only responsible for his own happiness, but also contributes to the common good, i.e. to the happiness of other people as well as to the well-being of animals and plants. The departure from ruthless egoism requires that people put their own needs (at least partially) aside and be interested in the welfare of their fellow human beings. Specifically, people will generally fight against suffering and injustice. If the common good is placed above the personal good, violence and crime will disappear. In future visions, community spirit is characterized by solidarity, love of neighbor and harmony.

Solidarity between the generations will be particularly pronounced in an ideal world. Each generation helps the others through its abilities. The older generation passes on its experience and knowledge to the younger one. In return, the younger generation uses its strength and energy to support older people in performing physical work and activities.

In addition to environmental issues, social injustice and equality were the most important topics for the students. For a large majority, there is no inequality and no injustice in their ideal world. Equality refers to all areas of life including work, health and education. They want their best possible world with social and financial justice and equal opportunities for all regardless of nationality, skin color, gender or sexual orientation. Their desire for justice and equality was motivated by the principle of fairness. Everyone should be treated fairly. If inequalities, racism and mutual mistrust were overcome, everyone could be happy. In the future, all people should go to school and receive training according to their abilities and interests, so that they can flourish in their profession and be happy.

> "My best possible future would be a world in which it is taken for granted that one eats healthily, cares for one's fellow human beings, in which it doesn't matter where one is born, in which one knows from the outset that people are different, have different cultures and habits but which one doesn't try to impose on anyone, but talks about them neutrally without making value judgments."

Justice also means overcoming global poverty. A key feature of a desirable future is the general well-being of humanity and the reduction of inequality between rich and poor. The focus is not on the material wealth of a few people, but on the individual and social well-being of the entire human race. Nobody would have to lose their life just because they are denied the basic rights to water and food. There would be more equality between countries because wealth and know-how would be distributed more fairly.

Justice also refers to the equal treatment of men and women, especially with regard to salaries and access to leadership positions. In the best possible world, women and men would have the same social rank and share the tasks of child care and professional development.

Another student wish was the rejection of nationalism with its tensions and conflicts, which are a consequence of competition and individualism. Instead of a policy of competition, alienation and isolation, one of integration and cohesion between the countries of this world was desirable. If the focus is on a solidarity-based coexistence between states, a harmonious world community can become a reality. But these great goals must already be implemented on a small scale. For many students, it was particularly important that no one is discriminated against or disadvantaged. Everyone should be accepted, respected and treated equally.

For the overwhelming majority of students, harmony in the form of mutual respect, a respectful coexistence, mutual helpfulness and a pronounced social behavior is one of the most important aspects of an ideal future. Harmony between economy and nature, harmony and appreciation between different cultures and nations as well as harmony between generations. Almost everyone has the need and the desire for a harmonious life with the environment and a harmonious and balanced togetherness with his fellow human beings and in harmony with nature. The desire for respect, tolerance and care for other people is very pronounced, i.e. foreigners, people of other skin color or confession, from other cultures and with different habits. Irrespective of their origin, religion and status in society, people meet with respect, esteem and on an equal footing.

"In my best possible world, the coexistence of humanity is characterized by harmony. The basis for this are the social relationships characterized by respect and tolerance as well as by mutual helpfulness and caring."

18.4 The Effect of Desirable Images of the Future

Following the two exercises on designing the best possible self and the best possible world, participants were able to reflect on their personal experiences, on the effect these exercises had on them, and on the value of these interventions. The key findings from this reflection are summarized and presented here.

With the exercises on the best possible future, the students were able to think about the big picture, about the problems of the present and the upcoming challenges, and about various aspects of quality of life and well-being. Many experienced the implementation of the exercises as a demanding, painful, and at the same time liberating process. Several of them admitted that the idea of a desirable future for themselves and the world was a real challenge for them. Some even felt overwhelmed at the beginning and had to abort the exercise several times because the idea of an ideal world seemed almost impossible. Sometimes they could not overcome current reality and free their imagination. Many found it difficult to deal with their future self because they were mainly occupied with the here and now in everyday life and hardly ever with the long-term future.

The common expectation that one must meet all requirements and present oneself as perfect and flawless also created a blockade in visualizing what one actually considered to be good and right. Only when one let go of such (false) ideas, opened oneself up to the hitherto unknown and could listen to one's intuition and inner voice, did the image of a fulfilled self and a livable world become imaginable at all. In some cases, the reflection on one's own future and on the future of the world and the resulting insights deeply influenced attitudes about one's own patterns of thought, about society and about one's personal role in it.

"It felt good to give myself this time out in the evening, to take a break from current reality and to enter a world for which I may still be too cowardly today. Imagining a future in which I have the courage to be myself and which makes my heart beat faster was really fascinating."

While designing an ideal future, many students experienced completely mixed emotions. For some of them, thinking about the future first caused fear and concern and triggered various negative emotions such as anger, sadness and powerlessness. Only as they were developing an ideal world in their minds did they become aware that we do not yet live in such a world and that values such as equality, justice and tolerance seem to be quite far off in many areas and in many parts of the world. Their lack of belief in the possibility of people and countries working together and committing themselves to the climate and environment made it difficult for them to imagine a better future.

"This exercise evokes a certain sadness because it shows me that the best possible world will remain a dream of humanity because the path to it requires renunciation, which humanity is not yet ready for."

Furthermore, the participants became aware of the target conflicts between future visions and the modern lifestyle. For example, the desire for intact nature and a sustainable lifestyle collides with the desire for consumption, prosperity and mobility. The discrepancy between how one ought to live and how one actually lives creates a cognitive dissonance that in turn generates a bad conscience and is hard to endure. However, these negative feelings also have a positive effect by shaking up a person and making them aware of the necessary changes in their lifestyle. The complexity and scope of the current problems and challenges became really clear only through these fields of tension. However, it was on the basis of these disturbing feelings that an honest and personal future vision could arise at all.

> "I particularly recommend the exercise of the 'best possible world' to people who have negative future expectations. In my opinion, the 'inner, pessimistic barrier' can be overcome by means of this exercise. Subsequently, positive impulses may arise which can contribute to increased motivation for future changes."

The students were challenged also because they had to think deliberately about their innermost values, wishes and life goals. The idea of an ideal future for oneself and the world was the first step towards the conscious alignment and orientation of one's own life. It made it possible to really get to know oneself, and to better understand what is really important and what one wants to achieve in life. The participants were able to think about their true values, passions and interests and what priorities they wanted to set in their everyday lives.

> "The described vision does not appear to me to be absurd, arbitrary, crazy or even unrealistic. I believe this may be because it is not completely foreign to me actually rather familiar, but estranged. I can imagine that I have visualized my yearnings or things that I have neglected or suppressed in the moment or so far. They are things and topics that excite me, but for which I hardly find or set aside more time in everyday life."

For example, material values were not given a high priority. Staying true to oneself is possible if values such as love of one's neighbor, helpfulness, family and minimalism instead of excessive consumption are emphasized. By not discriminating against anyone and behaving according to the principles of socially just and sustainable development, one moves closer to realizing one's personal and the general ideal state. Hence the participants reflected not only on what they wanted to achieve, but also on who they are today.

who they want to be in the future and what they can accomplish. They have thereby gained self-confidence, which has given them new courage and motivation for good decisions and initiatives in life.

"The possibility of contributing to the improvement of our world and accelerating the process of achieving my best possible world has created new energy and motivation within me."

The exercise was also valuable because the participants transferred themselves into the future not only cognitively and rationally, but also emotionally and imaginatively. The creative design of a desirable future scenario in the form of a colorful collage had a special effect. The resulting image could be internalized better through the use of artistic elements and thus a deeper connection could be established. By getting involved in the exercise creatively, the limits of one's own thinking could be overcome. One not only saw the desired ideal state in front of oneself, but could also sense it.

"It gave me great pleasure to let my creativity run free. It is important that we believe in our ability to shape the future world. We can already shape it by living according to the values that are important to us. The creative exercise helped me to realize what societal values I wish for our future world and that I would like to live according to them."

As a result, most of the participants then had more positive and uplifting feelings than negative and oppressive ones, as if new doors and perspectives were suddenly opening up for them. For some, an upward emotional spiral effect was even set into motion. Through the "forced" focus on the positive, the participants became step by step more open and optimistic. The idea of the best possible world was increasingly perceived as beautiful and encouraging. They suddenly felt joy and confidence. Through the idea of the best possible future, they became aware of how beautiful life and the world can be if you commit yourself to it.

The students came to the realization that wishful thinking and reality are not a contradiction in themselves and that utopias do not have to remain unattainable dreams. As soon as one trusts one's own feelings and intuition instead of ignoring them, the best possible future gets a whole new connection with reality. The design of an image of the ideal world was not at all experienced as naive and groundless fantasy. It opened the eyes for what is not working well at the moment and what the world should look like in the future. "Unrealistic" thinking is desired and valuable. Just think back 30 years: who would have considered mobile phones with internet and payment functions as realistic back then? Unrealistic does not mean impossible; it all depends on the faith and conviction with which one can move mountains and grow beyond oneself. Plans and goals that one does not believe in will hardly be achieved. It is precisely these "unrealistic" visions that effect progress and improve the quality of life.

> "I would be interested in knowing how quickly the world could improve if the tendency towards negative and pessimistic future visions were not so widespread. It is the task of all humanity to actively counter this trend. Therefore, not only politics should address such issues, but also parents at home and teachers at school."

Even if certain ideas seem utopian and unrealistic, they serve as inspiration and orientation for one's own behavior in order to achieve an ideal image. It is not possible to change the whole world, but one can contribute to change on a small scale. The visualization of this world created a previously unknown clarity for many and awakened a desire for personal commitment. All of a sudden abstract concepts such as community spirit became concrete and tangible because one could relate them to one's place of residence, to personal encounters with other people and to practical initiatives and projects. Only when concentrating on the image of a best possible world, do the chances and means for active participation became really conscious.

The engagement with positive visions of the future awakened in many students a desire to do something about it. Their interest was not about radical and pioneering changes that one has to push forward as a great leader. The participants recognized that hange is primarily about a fundamental awareness and modification of ideas, as well as often about small gestures and activities. The best thing is to focus on what one can influence oneself and not be discouraged by negative news from all over. Even if one's own contribution is humble. As soon as everyone thinks and acts together in the same direction, the world can be made a better place. If everyone does what is in their power, progress can be enormous.

In addition, many participants became aware that they can contribute much more than they previously suspected. It starts with rethinking one's own consumption behavior, such as eating less meat and avoiding unnecessary air travel, or only consuming products from companies that make a clear contribution to fair treatment of employees, suppliers and other business partners. Some even want to   professional focus on an area that contributes to the sustainable development of the earth. Others asked the question what their purpose in life and their contribution to this world might be. In conversations with colleagues, some even considered founding concrete sustainable projects.

> "As a result of this, my personal need to get involved in social projects in the future, for example to promote the education of children in developing countries, has increased during the exercise. Over time, I realized that the exercise made me more optimistic. This was shown by the fact that I was able to deal better with difficult situations because I had the long-term positive goal in mind."

In the end, what is important is consistent action according to one's ideals with respect to the world. As Mahatma Gandhi said: "Be the change you wish to see in the world." Only through our own behavior can we shape the world we long for. If we set an example to others by living according to our values, we will positively influence the world through our example and so change it step by step.

19

Living with Hope

In addition to the special wishes and ideals that we hope for, there is also a general, fundamental or radical hope that is of existential importance especially in times of crisis, uncertainty and disorientation. This fundamental hope differs from concrete hopes in that it is not oriented towards the realization of concrete and specific goals. Fundamental hope focuses on life as a whole and is independent of the realization of individual wishes. It refers to the deepest longing for a good, happy and fulfilling life.

19.1 Fundamental and Radical Hope

According to Blöser and Stahl (2017), fundamental hopes include those that determine our identity, i.e. the way we see ourselves. The hope of parents for their children is such an example. Parents want and must hope for their children so that they can regard themselves as good parents (Hinds et al., 2009). This type of hope is valuable in itself because it defines the way people shape their lives. With the loss of this fundamental hope, we would also lose part of our identity. If we lose our faith and trust in our children, we feel as if we have failed as parents. This can, for example, also explain why seriously ill patients can still hope despite a negative prognosis. Their dignity and identity are connected with the hope of life. But this also applies to less existential cases. A footballer hopes (at least as a striker) to score goals, a firefighter hopes to be able to extinguish fires, and a chef hopes to be able to prepare a good dish. As soon as the striker no longer scores goals, the firefighter no longer extinguishes fires and the chef no longer cooks good dishes, they stop being a striker, a firefighter and a (good) chef. By giving up their hopes, these people lose an important part of their identity.

If we invert the argument, this means that by choosing certain wishes and hopes, we simultaneously choose what person we want to be. Such fundamental hope is about the self-conception, self-awareness and self-worth of the hoping person themselves. We consciously or unconsciously take on a certain identity and its associated values and hopes. Once we give up these hopes, whether because they are no longer important to us or because we no longer believe in their realization, our self-conception and our identity change. Giving up these fundamental hopes can be a natural process of development (for example, a person changes their profession from "musician" to "lawyer") or trigger an identity crisis if someone takes on an identity whose hopes cannot be realized.

In addition to the special wishes and ideals we hope for, there is also a general, fundamental or radical hope in life that is of existential importance especially in times of crisis, uncertainty and disorientation. This fundamental hope differs from concrete hopes in that it is not oriented towards the realization of concrete and specific goals. Fundamental hope aims at life as a whole and is independent of the realization of individual wishes. It refers to the deepest longing for a good, happy and fulfilling life.

With a hopeful attitude in life, we are open and attentive to new possibilities and are not oppressed by current obstacles and difficulties. This makes hope resistant to short-term disappointments. Fundamental hope is a quality that supports us when individual hopes fail. Even if some hopes can end in disappointment (which is often the case), the power of fundamental hope lies in the fact that we can always find new meaning and thus new hope in life. At the moment when particular hopes fail, a deeper ability to hope protects us from a general sense of helplessness and hopelessness, gives us support and enables us to hold out in difficult times. Just as fear and worry can become a habit, also hope can grow into a general attitude with respect to life and the future (Shade, 2001).

Of particular importance is also "radical" hope. Jonathan Lear (2009) describes radical hope as a hope that takes us in critical and crisis-ridden life situations beyond the limits of what we have known. Radical hope is openness to new and previously unimagined possibilities. In unfamiliar and extreme situations we look for completely new ways. We look for leadership, enlightenment, inspiration or strength to lead us through difficult times. Radical hope therefore arises when the previous framework of meaning and significance is lost and one sets one's hopes on a transcendent power. This hope is also radical because the future for which one hopes exceeds one's own imagination. If Lear is right, we can certainly hope for things that at the moment we cannot yet imagine. This is a kind of hope that can survive the loss of all individual hopes and that make us open and receptive to unknown possibilities. We do not know how we will get out of a certain situation, but we can still believe and trust that it will somehow be possible.

19.2 Hope in the Present for the Present

Hope is omnipresent in life and therefore we hardly notice it. Probably we do not recognize the value of hope in our daily life because it is as omnipresent and self-evident as air for us humans or water for fish. That is why one also says "where there is life, there is hope". If we live with hope, we live with an interest in how our life and that of others will develop. Things are not all the same to us; rather we care about how life unfolds and how our ideas and plans as well as those of other people develop. If we lose this fundamental hope, life becomes meaningless (Callina et al., 2018).

This kind of hope is not about a vision of the future, but rather about a way of living in the present. In this sense, we can hope in and for the present and not only in the present for a distant future (Herth & Cutcliffe, 2002). We all hope more or less for the preservation of health, for a happy marriage, family or partnership, for a harmonious life, for good relationships with other people, for self-determination and for a meaningful purpose in life (see Sect. 15.2). Hope is thus connected to association with other people and is not determined by the realization of future events. The following saying probably expresses this kind of hope best: "As long as we are healthy and together with our loved ones, we are ready for anything that might happen."

As Benzein and his colleagues (Benzein et al., 2001) have recognized, hope as an inner force can be aimed at our life in the here and now. This deeper feeling of hope in life is much more than the hopes we have in specific situations. There is therefore a difference between "hoping for something" and "living with hope". We do not necessarily have to hope for a material goal. Often it is enough to simply live hopefully. We are hopeful people when we wish for a good, fulfilling and shared life, and believe and trust that this is also possible. In this sense, hope is less focused on future-oriented goals than on a state that extends from the present into the future.

Hope is an essential part of our lives because with hope we can have a better and richer life that is oriented towards more comprehensive values. A life without hope would, as McGeer (2004) emphasizes, actually not be a human life. Hope is a life-sustaining psychological resource. Thanks to the hope we have in and for the present, we can get out of bed in the morning, look forward to the new day, do our work and lead our lives to the best of our ability. Without it, there is little that could keep us on our feet, which is the reason that we must not give up hope even in the bleakest situations (Lazarus, 1999).

Living with hope means that no matter what the day brings us, we are grateful for every experience and have the confidence to deal with every problem positively. ope in the present keeps us open for the immediate experiences and surprises of everyday life. It focuses on being and less on doing, although of course one has to do something to maintain a positive state. It is a general orientation towards life and the future that determines how we react to the trials of life and thereby shape the present. In this way we remain open to new experiences and espouse the belief that we can overcome adversities and change life to our advantage. This type of hope, Shade (2001) writes, requires mental flexibility and emotional resilience. It is resistant to disappointment and adapts goals and means to the given circumstances.

Unlike directed hope, general hope lies in the meaning that is attributed to life (Parker-Oliver, 2002). Hope is a prerequisite for a meaningful human life and action. We become hopeless when we no longer understand the world around us, when the world no longer makes sense to us, when everything that we do no longer has meaning. Here, hope is characterized primarily by a positive attitude towards life. Meaning and hope are interwoven because hope is the prerequisite for a meaningful life on the one hand, and meaning in life is the basis for a hopeful attitude on the other. The hopeful person confers meaning on the current situation and draws inner strength from it. As the former Czech President Václav Havel once said:

"Hope is not the conviction that something will turn out well but the certainty that something makes sense, regardless of how it turns out. (…) The more I think about it, the more I incline to the opinion that the most important thing of all is not to lose hope and faith in life itself. Anyone who does so is lost, regardless of what good fortune may befall him. On the other hand, those who do not lose it can never come to a bad end. This doesn't mean closing one's eyes to the horrors of the world—quite the contrary, in fact: only those who have not lost faith and hope can see the horrors of the world with genuine clarity." (Havel, 1990, p. 141).

19.3 Hope and Personal Growth

Life is not static, but instead means change, development, and growth. Hope, for Rorty (1999), is the prerequisite and condition for all growth. Hope enables us to undergo a creative transformation. The attitude of hope, as Marcel (1949) says, is a mysterious force with which we can confront adversities in life and overcome dark times. Hope is not an escape from current circumstances, but rather their conquest and transformation. The power of hope lies in the ability to change the world (and ourselves) for the better, rather than to escape it.

According to Shade (2001), we need to understand hope in life as a process of development. A hopeful life is a life of growth and personal and social progress. By hoping, we strengthen, develop, and transform our basic abilities while expanding our horizons and enriching our lives. Hope does not only refer to our current abilities, but is the driving force for the further development of our strengths and a substantial trust in our potential. We can observe this most clearly in children. Children explore not only their environment, but also their own abilities. When we give our children basic trust, we support their hope, strengthen their belief in themselves, and promote the expansion of their action repertoire.

Shade (2001) describes the nature of hope as one of conditional transcendence. Hope is conditional because it arises from our current life circumstances, but it is also a form of transcendence because, through the phenomenon of hope, we can overcome the current situation and the accompanying limitations and not be trapped in them. What is decisive for hope is the constant overcoming of negative emotions such as disappointment, frustration and discouragement. Hope can be understood as a form of leaping, overcoming, growing and expanding. Hope transforms us and leads us beyond the current conditions. Thanks to hope, we tap into previously unknown energy sources. Even if it means going beyond our conditions and abilities, we involve ourselves with the desirability and feasibility of a better future. By hoping and taking on new hopes, we expand our horizon, shift our boundaries, find new opportunities and create new strengths and conditions through our commitment and trust.

The heart of hope, as Shade (2001) says, is born in the intimacy of concrete relationships and opens up new horizons that extend beyond the limits of our current conditions and limitations. Hoping is an activity that promotes individual and collective growth through helping and supporting one another. We grow through bonding with and trusting other people. We can expand our sphere of influence and promote the realization of our hopes by standing together with others. Hope therefore means overcoming limiting factors through cooperation and collaboration.

Hope is essentially the way we expand the self through relationships with others, be it through thoughts or deeds. With the energy and power of hope we shape our lives and the world. We do not content ourselves with the current state, but strive for more, for a better state for ourselves and for others. By hoping, we explore with our imagination what we can achieve in life and what can still happen in the world and in the lives of other people. Our awareness and our horizon expand, and we are curious and open to new ideas and possibilities that can be realized together with other people. In this way we grow beyond our own limitations and expand our powers.

For McGeer (2004), hope can be unconditional in a certain sense. In unconditional love (as in the love for our children), we give other people our unconditional and unending hope. The basis for this, in addition to love, is a fundamental belief and trust in the valuable uniqueness and creative power of the other person. Through unconditional hope we believe and trust absolutely in a successful life for the beloved person.

20

Developing Hope

Our lives, as we live them every day, are determined by conscious and unconscious habits. These habits reflect our preferences and previous experiences. They arise in the social context of family, friends, school and work and develop into general and often unquestioned matters of course. Unfortunately, not all of our habits are positive and advantageous for a successful and fulfilling life. Phenomena such as negative thoughts, prejudices, worries, criticism and lack of self-confidence are often inhibiting and almost insurmountable habits that cloud our view of the future and our hope. These need to be overcome and replaced by positive habits. The habits of hope include openness to new things, creativity, courage, determination, commitment, perseverance, but also patience, solidarity, helpfulness and, above all, a belief in the goodness of people and trust in ourselves and in others.

20.1 The Power of Habit

In order to develop our capacity to hope, we need to throw certain negative habits overboard and acquire positive habits. Dewey (1922) shows in his philosophy that a large part of our ordinary human behavior is not thought out or planned at all, but rather consists of habits. In our habits certain preferences and dislikes are reflected that were influenced by earlier experiences and activities. Even though habits are automated to a certain extent and function unconsciously, they are nevertheless actions that are carried out voluntarily. Habits arise from an active decision what one wants to do regularly in everyday life. But as soon as one has grown fond of certain habits and they have become anchored in everyday life, they proceed unconsciously and shape one's character.

A. M. Krafft, *Our Hopes, Our Future*, https://doi.org/10.1007/978-3-662-66205-2_20

Habits are not purely individual, but arise in a social context. We acquire our habits through contact and interaction with other people. In particular, habits arise through imitation of earlier habits. For example, children take on the habits of their parents and so carry them on. In this respect, certain habits can be inherited so to speak, i.e. passed on through socialization. If several people are confronted with the same situations and react to them in a similar way, collective habits arise which develop into social patterns.

Habits consist of behaviour carried out routinely, and over time disregard conscious reflection on goals and purposes. But in life circumstances change so that certain habits become useless or even harmful. The question then arises if one can alter the earlier habits and acquire new ones. Since we humans build an emotional bond with our habits and thus gain security, our habits are usually difficult to change, especially if they are associated with prevailing social norms.

For this reason, Dewey relies on the development of positive habits in the education of young people. Children and adolescents have not yet developed rigid habits and can, through independent thinking, critical questioning, creative experimentation and thanks to their imagination and empathy for others, acquire good habits for shaping the future. But what are those negative habits that hinder our ability to hope, and what are the good ones that make us hopeful?

20.2 Overcoming Negative Habits

Our thinking and acting is often characterized by unreflected habits and a lack of mindfulness and appreciation. Some of our habits fall among the inhibiting conditions of our hope. Bad habits limit our hope and cause us to fall back into old patterns. Among the negative habits are, for example, a lack of belief in ourselves, the fears and worries with which we look into the future, and our negative thoughts and beliefs.

Bad habits are related to our perception, attention and emotional involvement. In a wide-ranging literature review, Baumeister and his colleagues found that we often pay more attention to negative events than to positive ones (Baumeister et al., 2001). Threatening phenomena are more consciously and more intensely perceived than pleasant ones. Critical information is processed more thoroughly than an already familiar one. Bad behavior remains more frequently and longer in our memory than good behavior. Negative experiences have a stronger emotional effect than positive ones. This can basically be explained by the evolution of man: in order for man to survive, he had to recognize threatening signals faster and estimate possible negative consequences in order to be able to react correctly. Out of this necessity arose certain habits in our perception, information processing and memory which helped us to grasp negative situations faster and better.

The consequence of this is that we usually deal more with problems and other negative elements because we automatically focus our attention on errors (Klinger et al., 1980). Bad news in the media is received more attentively than good news, generates stronger emotions and also remains longer in our memory. We talk more often about bad things like diseases, accidents and mishaps than we do about good things. We think longer about defeats than about successes (Gilovich, 1983). The negative properties and behaviors of other people catch our eye more quickly than their positive character traits. Stereotypes about other people and ethnic groups are mostly negative because negative experiences contribute more to an overall impression than positive features do (Mullen & Johnson, 1990). We also tend to judge others more quickly as bad than as good. Negative feedback and criticism are given more often and leave a stronger impression than positive feedback and recognition (Vonk, 1999). As a result of these phenomena, further bad habits arise, e.g. prejudice, envy, selfishness, competition and confrontation.

But for most people the good outweighs the bad in life. The good is part of everyday life and the bad is rather the exception (Baumeister et al., 2001). In addition, most people believe in the good in life, at least implicitly. In the course of our lives, we usually have many more positive experiences than negative ones, but we do not always perceive them equally well. Thus an imbalance arises between our positive experiences and our negative feelings and habits. We actually feel good, but we still have to scold, gossip and complain. This negative thinking and talking then develops into a complaint that unnecessarily makes our lives difficult and in many cases even causes illness.

As long as one focuses on the negative aspects of life and of people, one will not be able to have much hope for the future. If people hold a negative view of the world and of people, they will hardly be able to convey hope to others (Krafft, 2019). Fear and worry can shake us up, but they can also limit and hold us captive. The danger of fear and worry is that they can paralyze us instead of encouraging us to act. We should not run away from real problems, but we must also not become prisoners of fear and worry, but rather open ourselves up to hope.

Characteristic of hope is that it is particularly needed in times of adversity and suffering. Hope only becomes really relevant where there is doubt, suffering and need. Wherever there is fear, there is usually also a glimmer of hope. Through hope, an integration of the positive and negative aspects of life takes place, the interrelationships and interactions of which we need to become aware so that personal development can take place. With hope, we can understand the positive in connection with the negative and in the process focus over and over again on the positive, thereby conveying a positive view of things to our fellow human beings.

20.3 Nurturing Positive Habits

In practical terms, according to Shade (2001), hope is characterized by a set of habits that orient us towards a better future and encourage us to act. Habits of hope are the means and activities that strengthen our ability to hope and lead to realization of our individual and collective hopes. We can develop new habits of growth and social progress and focus our energy on goodness both in the present and in future possibilities. Positive habits can generate new power for the realization of our hopes, promote growth and expand our lives rather than constrict them. These include habits such as ingenuity and openness to new possibilities, belief goodness, and confidence in oneself and others. Hope also requires courage, willpower and commitment, but also perseverance, patience, humility and tranquility. Finally, hope is based on mutual solidarity and helpfulness (Kadlac, 2015; Krafft, 2019; Shade, 2001; Stitzlein, 2019). These habits of hope can strengthen our character and let us become a hopeful person.

Openness to new things and inventiveness
With hope comes an openness to new ways and valuable future possibilities. Inventiveness and imagination support us in actively forming new ways and means and and in overcoming obstacles. In order for us to pursue and realize our hopes, we need to use our inventiveness and sometimes even to expand it. Thanks to our imagination and creativity, we can broaden our sense of what and how something can be possible. We explore alternatives and find resources and means that bring about new options. We can imagine meaningful future scenarios and experiment inventively with new solutions.

New technologies can on the whole increase our resources and give us access to a wider range of options. During the COVID-19 pandemic we were able to further develop our use of digital media and to experience its benefits. Hope is generally an attitude of openness and positive orientation towards the future, regardless of whether our specific hopes are fulfilled or not. This gives us energy and connects us with other people.

Commitment, perseverance and patience

A committed and patient hope is the opposite of indifference and resignation (McDonald, 2008). In the face of difficulties and setbacks, commitment to a worthy goal is maintained through perseverance and persistence. If our hopes are still beyond our current possibilities, patience is also required. When we hope, we connect patience with an active orientation towards our goals. Through perseverance and patience, we can overcome impatience and discouragement and hold fast on to our hopes.

As soon as impatience arises, we tend to give up our hopes too early. Patience is an ability through which we maintain our awareness, focus on our hopes and at the same time give things time to develop in the way that is best. Through patience we can wait for the right time for the fulfillment of our hopes and possibly for appropriate help from outside. Unlike passive or resigned waiting, we focus our attention and energy on the realization of our hopes when we actively wait. Hopeful endurance is a mixture of patiently waiting for the right moment and maintaining our interest and commitment so that we can stay active and move forward as soon as the opportunity arises.

Patience also includes humility and trust in the support of other people. Humility lets us recognize our present limits and makes us receptive to the abilities of other people or a higher power that we can actively seek and gratefully accept. By requesting and receiving help from other people, we humbly recognize our own limits, our vulnerability and our dependence on others.

The humility and patience of hope also bring a feeling of calm and inner peace comes in critical situations. As is well known, power lies in peace. People who become restless and in turn stir up unrest become hectic and nervous, isolate themselves and remain alone. Those who can keep the peace will be more open and receptive to unexpected things. Especially fundamental and radical hope arises when we are at peace and in harmony with ourselves and the world.

Courage, determination and willpower

Hope also requires courage, determination and willpower. By hoping, we expose ourselves to setbacks and disappointments that require that we be determined and show willpower. We need willpower especially in bad times when we feel frustrated, demotivated, even desperate and are about to throw in the towel and give everything up.

In this context, courage is required because when we hope, we have to take risks, let ourselves open up to an uncertain future and accept potential disappointments. We therefore need to hold on to our wishes and believe in their realization even though we are fully aware of the uncertainty of the future and the possibility of failure. This requires a courageous hope, for it would be an easy thing to hope only when we can assume that our wishes will be fulfilled for sure.

Courage flourishes in many ways in hope: we courageously recognize our limits and ask others for help; we become aware of our vulnerability and dependence; but we also stand up for unpopular issues if we are convinced of them; when we are disappointed, we stay on course and persevere. By realizing our hopes, we courageously change our lives.

We develop courage and determination whenever our hopes are particularly important to us. Unlike with optimism, with hope we recognize the obstacles and risks involved. Nevertheless, we are not intimidated by them, but go courageously forward. With courage we can face the fears and worries as well as the uncertainty and difficulties encountered on the way to fulfilling our hopes.

Solidarity and willingness to help

The uncertainty of the future, the unpredictability and difficulties in fulfilling our hopes often require us to cooperate with other people. In order to achieve our goals, we often have to rely on the collaboration and support of others. Cohesion and willingness to help are the opposites of selfishness and competition.

In hoping we are open and available to other people. They can trust us and count on our willingness to help and support them. Solidarity is most evident when we face challenges together while realizing the hopes that are dear to us all. When this happens, the content of our hopes is important because we develop greater solidarity when we desire the same future and actively work to realize it. This recognizes the mutual dependence we have on each other.

Belief in goodness

Hope is fundamentally linked to believing in goodness. If one did not believe in goodness, one would not be able to hope. Hope is sustained by a belief in the good within ourselves, in other people, and in the world. Hope for a better world is founded on the belief in the goodness of the world, that things will take a good turn.

Hope is based on a belief in the possibility of a better life and on trust in other people. Belief in the good in life is a prerequisite for serious commitment to a better world. Even if we do not always understand the present and cannot foresee the future, belief in our own abilities together with belief in the abilities and goodwill of others will maintain hope for a better world.

Often hope implies belief in a higher power that lies beyond our control. In order to maintain hope, we sometimes have to believe in a transcendent entity (nature, luck, fate, God, etc.). For many people, hope depends on belief in the love, goodness, or care of such a higher entity. This also includes a belief in the new possibilities that the future offers us.

Conclusion: Hope for Shaping the Future

The future is not something that just happens to us and to which we are exposed for better or worse. We can and must actively and constructively shape our future. For that what matters most is our willpower. But then we need to know what we really and from the bottom of our hearts want, what is most important to us in life; and finally, we need to believe that we can achieve our goals.

This is where the importance of a meaningful life comes in. The feeling of meaninglessness is one of the greatest sources of suffering in life. Every person who hopes for a good future hopes for something that is meaningful and valuable to him. Only through the experience of a sense in life can a person remain hopeful even difficult times. The deepest meaning in life, according to Viktor Frankl, is self-transcendent. This meaning points beyond our own life and lies in the commitment to a good cause or in a willingness to help other people. The more a person grasps his responsibilities, the more meaningful his life will seem to him and the more hopeful he will feel. People who have meaningful work experience what they do as valuable and rewarding, are therefore more goal-oriented, and feel that their life has a deeper meaning, which is why they also look to the future more positively.

A hope filled with meaning is linked to the conviction that we can make the best of our lives in positive and painful times alike. Meaning-centered hope is based on the inviolable freedom of the human being, which allows him to overcome any disappointment and to experience a deeper meaning in every adverse situation, to affirm life and to remain hopeful. For this there are three basic prerequisites: 1. a positive attitude towards all life situations, whether we like them or not; 2. the creative development of new

A. M. Krafft, *Our Hopes, Our Future*, https://doi.org/10.1007/978-3-662-66205-2

possibilities in a given situation; 3. the freedom and the will to seize these possibilities and to realize them. Meaning and hope are not found in an indefinite future, but are based on the recognition of the moment when one reflects on values such as gratitude, attentiveness, forgiveness, justice and reconciliation.

In a changing world, the will to create, the ability to act and the willingness to help of each and every individual counts. The future is a space full of creative possibilities which, however, need to be identified and grasped together. Positive change does not happen by itself. As a society, we need to find creative solutions, but also grow beyond ourselves by throwing old habits overboard and following new paths. For this we need visions of the future that go beyond past and present life forms and encourage society to transform itself in new directions. Therefore, every individual should think about his or her personal hopes, i.e. what is particularly important to him or her in life, what his or her ideal is and how it can be achieved.

However, this does not mean that we always have to do everything alone and with our limited strength. Current events often push us to the limits of our own possibilities and abilities. They teach us how to turn to other people, trust them and accept their help. That is the great power of hope. By becoming aware of the great problems and challenges of our time and accepting them as opportunities for growth, we can believe in a good future and at the same time trust that, thanks to our own strengths and together with other people, we will be able to solve the problems and overcome the obstacles so that our most ardent wishes will finally come true. We can look forward to the next upheavals in the history of mankind and, full of hope, participate in shaping a better future in the midst of all adversities.

Appendix

Demographic structure of the samples

	2019		2020	
	Number	%	Number	%
Total	10.907	100	10.230	100
Countries				
Australia	474	4.3	210	2.1
France	94	0.9	235	2.3
India	1092	10.0	272	2.7
Israel	884	8.1	228	2.2
Italy	272	2.5	406	4.0
Colombia	311	2.9	222	2.2
Malta	148	1.4	149	1.5
Nigeria	665	6.1	210	2.1
Austria	–	–	244	2.4
Poland	481	4.4	227	2.2
Portugal	507	4.6	567	5.5
Switzerland (total)	3935	36.1	6968	68.1
– German	(2195)	(20.1)	(4205)	(41.1)
– French	(1502)	(13.8)	(1904)	(18.6)
– Italian	(238)	(2.2)	(859)	(8.4)
Spain	529	4.9	112	1.1
South Africa	1046	9.6	133	1.3
Czech Republic	469	4.3	257	2.5
Gender				
Male	4529	41.5	3678	36.0
Female	6378	58.5	6552	64.0
Age				
18–29	3679	33.7	2267	22.1
30–39	2098	19.2	1747	17.1
40–49	1896	17.4	1975	19.3

© The Editor(s) (if applicable) and The Author(s), under exclusive license to Springer-Verlag GmbH, DE, part of Springer Nature 2022
A. M. Krafft, *Our Hopes, Our Future*, https://doi.org/10.1007/978-3-662-66205-2

	2019		2020	
	Number	%	Number	%
50–59	1780	16.3	2228	21.8
60–69	1054	9.7	1476	14.4
70–79	366	3.4	475	4.6
80+	34	0.3	62	0.6
Highest education				
No completed school education	85	0.8	60	0.6
Primary school/elementary school completed	274	2.5	269	2.6
Specialized school without A-levels/ without university entrance qualification	508	4.7	511	5.0
High School	2153	19.7	1899	18.6
Vocational / Professional training	2889	26.5	2787	27.2
Higher vocational training with diploma	2235	20.5	2667	26.1
College/University	2615	24.0	1809	16.5
No information	148	1.4	228	2.2
Family status				
Still living with parents	2051	18.8	1223	12.0
Single, unmarried	1742	16.0	1358	13.3
In a partnership, but living separately	606	5.6	628	6.1
Living together in a partnership	1442	13.2	1741	17.0
Married	4116	37.7	4060	39.7
Divorced/separated	787	7.2	784	7.7
Widowed	163	1.5	208	2.0
No answer			228	2.2
Children				
No children	5676	52.0	4718	46.1
One or more children	5231	48.0	5284	51.7
No information			228	2.2
Main activity				
In training	2256	20.7	1142	11.2
Household work/child care	434	4.0	419	4.1
Part-time employment	1572	14.4	1977	19.3
Full-time employment	4887	44.8	4304	42.1
Unemployed/jobless	603	5.5	441	4.3
Retirement (age or illness)	1007	9.2	1316	12.9
No information	148	1.4	631	6.2
Occupational status				
No position in a professional organization	1958	18.0	1777	17.4
In training	1699	15.6	838	8.2
Employee	3703	34.0	3597	35.2
Junior/Middle Management	1551	14.2	1646	16.1
Senior Management/Executive/ Board of directors	666	6.1	613	6.0

	2019		2020	
	Number	%	Number	%
Owner/independent	1182	10.8	1128	11.0
No information	148	1.4	631	6.2
Religion				
Catholic	3159	29.0	3191	31.2
Protestant or Lutheran	1139	10.4	1505	14.7
Other Christian church or other Christian confession	932	8.5	388	3.8
Islam	349	3.2	125	1.2
Judaism	538	4.9	261	2.5
Hinduism	568	5.2	225	2.2
Buddhism	62	0.6	73	0.7
I am a spiritual person outside of traditional world religions	1278	11.7	974	9.5
Without religion, without confession or withdrawn	2456	22.5	3181	31.1
Something else	426	3.9	307	3.0

References

Armeli, S., Gunthert, K. C., & Cohen, L. H. (2001). Stressor appraisals, coping, and post-event outcomes: The dimensionality and antecedents of stress-related growth. *Journal of Social and Clinical Psychology, 20*(3), 366–395.

Aspinwall, L. G. (2005). The psychology of future-oriented thinking: From achievement to proactive coping, adaptation, and aging. *Motivation and Emotion, 29*(4), 203–235.

Auderset, J., & Moser, P. (2012). Krisenerfahrungen, Lernprozesse und Bewältigungsstrategien. Die Ernährungskrise von 1917/18 als agrarpolitische „Lehrmeisterin". In T. David, J. Mathieu, J. Schaufelbuehl, & T. Straumann (Hrsg.), *Krisen: Ursachen, Deutungen und Folgen. Schweizerisches Jahrbuch für Wirtschafts- und Sozialgeschichte, 27* (S. 133–150). Chronos Verlag.

Baumeister, R. F., & Masicampo, E. J. (2010). Conscious thought is for facilitating social and cultural interactions: How mental simulations serve the animal-culture interface. *Psychological Review, 117,* 945–971.

Baumeister, R. F., & Tice, D. M. (1985). Toward a theory of situational structure. *Environment and Behavior, 17*(2), 147–192.

Baumeister, R. F., Bratslavsky, E., Finkenauer, C., & Vohs, K. D. (2001). Bad is stronger than good. *Review of General Psychology, 5*(4), 323–370.

Baumeister, R. F., Vohs, K. D., Aaker, J. L., & Garbinsky, E. N. (2013). Some key differences between a happy life and a meaningful life. *The Journal of Positive Psychology, 8,* 505–516.

Baumeister, R. F., Hofmann, W., Summerville, A., & Vohs, K. D. (2016a). *Everyday thoughts about the past, present, and future: Studies of mental time travel.* Department of Psychology, Florida State University.

Baumeister, R. F., Vohs, K. D., & Oettingen, G. (2016b). Pragmatic prospection: How and why people think about the future. *Review of General Psychology, 20*(1), 3–16.

Baumeister, R. F., Maranges, H. M., & Sjåstad, H. (2018). Consciousness of the future as a matrix of maybe: Pragmatic prospection and the simulation of alternative possibilities. *Psychology of Consciousness: Theory, Research, and Practice, 5*(3), 223–238.

Benzein, E., Norberg, A., & Saveman, B. I. (2001). The meaning of the lived experience of hope in patients with cancer in palliative home care. *Palliative Medicine, 15*(2), 117–126.

Bell, W. (1997). The purposes of futures studies. *The Futurist, 31*(6), 42.

Bell, W. (2009). *Foundations of futures studies: History, purposes, knowledge. Volume I: Human Science for a New Era.* Transaction Publishers.

Bühler, G., Craviolini, J., Krähenbühl, D., Hermann, M., Müller, E., & Wenger, V. (2020). *Generationen-Barometer.* Berner Generationenhaus & SOTOMO.

Billias, N. (2010). Hope as a moral virtue. In J. McDonald & A. M. Stephenson (Hrsg.), *The resilience of hope* (S. 17–27). Brill Rodopi.

Bloch, E. (1959). *Das Prinzip Hoffnung. In fünf Teilen.* Suhrkamp TB.

Blöser, C., & Stahl, T. (2017). Fundamental hope and practical identity. *Philosophical Papers, 46*(3), 345–371.

Blöser, C., & Stahl, T. (Hrsg.). (2019). *The moral psychology of hope. Rowman & littlefield international.* Chapter 1 An Introduction, 1–11.

Bostrom, N., & Yudkowsky, E. (2014). The ethics of artificial intelligence. *The Cambridge Handbook of Artificial Intelligence, 1,* 316–334.

Boulding, E. (1994). Image and action in peace building. In D. Hicks (Hrsg.), *Preparing for the future: Notes & queries for concerned educators* (S. 61–84). Adamantine Press.

Braithwaite, J. (2004a). Emancipation and hope. *The Annals of the American Academy of Political and Social Science, 592*(1), 79–98.

Braithwaite, V. (2004b). Collective hope. *The Annals of the American Academy of Political and Social Science, 592*(1), 6–15.

Braithwaite, V. (2004c). The hope process and social inclusion. *The Annals of the American Academy of Political and Social Science, 592*(1), 128–151.

Brunstad, P. O. (2002). Longing for belonging: Youth culture in Norway. In J. Gidley, N. Ingwersen, & S. Inayatullah (Hrsg.), *Youth futures: Comparative research and transformative visions* (S. 143–154). Greenwood.

Bovens, L. (1999). The value of hope. *Philosophy and Phenomenological Research, 59*(3), 667–681.

Burke, P. (2012). Does hope have a history? *Estudos Avançados, 26,* 207–218.

Calhoun, C. (2018). *Doing valuable time: The present, the future, and meaningful living.* Oxford University Press.

Callina, K. S., Snow, N., & Murray, E. D. (2018). The history of philosophical and psychological perspectives on hope: Toward defining hope for the science of positive human development. In M. Gallagher & S. Lopez (Hrsg.), *The Oxford handbook of hope* (S. 9–26). Oxford University Press.

Carver, C. S., Scheier, M. F., & Weintraub, J. K. (1989). Assessing coping strategies: A theoretically based approach. *JJournal of Personality and Social Psychology, 56*(2), 267–283.

Cohen, S., Kamarck, T., & Mermelstein, R. (1983). A global measure of perceived stress. *Journal of Health and Social Behavior, 24*(4), 385–396.

Cohen, S., Kessler, R. C., & Gordon, L. U. (Hrsg.). (1997). *Measuring stress: A guide for health and social scientists.* Oxford University Press on Demand.

Collins, R., Taylor, S., & Skokan, L. (1990). A better world or a shattered vision: Changes in life perspectives following victimization. *Social Cognition, 8,* 263–265.

Costanza, R., & Kubiszewski, I. (2014) Why we need visions of a sustainable and desirable world. In R. Costanza & I. Kubiszewski, I. (Hrsg.), *Creating a sustainable and desirable future: Insights from 45 global thought leaders.* World Scientific.

Cornish, E. (2001). Three paradoxes of time. *The Futurist, 35*(4), 32.

Cristea, I. A., Sucala, M., Stefan, S., Igua, R., David, D., & Tatar, A. (2011). Positive and negative emotions in cardiac patients: The contributions of trait optimism, expectancies and hopes. *Cognition, Brain, Behaviour, 15*(3), 317–329.

Cyranowski, J. M., Zill, N., Bode, R., Butt, Z., Kelly, M. A., Pilkonis, P. A., Salsman, J., & Cella, D. (2013). Assessing social support, companionship, and distress: National Institute of Health (NIH) toolbox adult social relationship scales. *Health Psychology, 32*(3), 293–301.

Dalferth, I. U. (2016). *Hoffnung.* de Gruyter.

Dator, J. (1996). Futures studies as applied knowledge. In R. Slaughter (Hrsg.), *New thinking for a new millennium.* Routledge.

David, D., Montgomery, G. H., Stan, R., DiLorenzo, T., & Erblich, J. (2004). Discrimination between hopes and expectancies for nonvolitional outcomes: Psychological phenomenon or artifact? *Personality and Individual Differences, 36*(8), 1945–1952.

David, D., Montgomery, G., & DiLorenzo, T. (2006). Response expectancy versus response hope in predicting distress. A brief research report. *Erdelyi Pszichologiai Szemle, 1,* 1–13.

David, T., Mathieu, J., Schaufelbuehl, J. M., & Straumann, T. (2012). *Krisen: Ursachen, Deutungen und Folgen. Schweizerisches Jahrbuch für Wirtschafts- und Sozialgeschichte, 27.* Chronos Verlag.

de Quervain, D., Aerni, A., Amini, E., Bentz, D., Coynel, D., Gerhards, C., Fehlmann, B., Freytag, V., Papassotiropoulos, A., Schicktanz, N., Schlitt, T., Zimmer, A., & Zuber, P. (2020). *The Swiss corona stress study.* Report of the University of Basel.

Dewey, J. (1922). *Human nature and conduct: An introduction to social psychology.* Henry Holt and Co.

Dewey, J. (1980). Democracy and education. Project Gutenberg. https://www.fulltextarchive.com/pdfs/Democracy-and-Education.pdf. (Erstveröffentlichung 1916).

Eckersley, R. (1995). Values and visions: Youth and the failure of modern western culture. *Youth Studies Australia, 14*(1), 13–21.

Eckersley, R. (1999). Dreams and expectations: Young people's expected and preferred futures and their signifcance for education. *Futures, 31*(1), 73–90.

Eckersley, R. (2002). Future visions, social realities, and private lives: Young people and their personal well-being. In J. Gidley, N. Ingwersen, & S. Inayatullah (Hrsg.), *Youth futures: Comparative research and transformative visions* (S. 31–42). Greenwood.

Eckersley, R., Cahill, H., Wierenga, A., & Wyn, J. (2007). *Generations in dialogue about the future: The hopes and fears of young Australians.* Australia 21 Ltd. Australian Youth Research Centre.

Elgin, D. (1991). Creating a sustainable future. *ReVision, 14*(2), 77–79.

Erikson, E. (1998). *Jugend und Krise: Die Psychodynamik im sozialen Wandel.* Klett-Cotta.

Felder, C. (2018). *Die Gemeinwohlökonomie.* Deuticke Verlag.

Frankl, V. E. (1979). *Der Mensch vor der Frage nach dem Sinn – Eine Auswahl aus dem Gesamtwerk.* Piper.

Fredrickson, B. L. (2013). Positive emotions broaden and build. *Advances in Experimental Social Psychology, 47*(1), 1–53.

Gidley, J. M. (2017). *The future: A very short introduction.* Oxford University Press.

Gilbert, D., & Wilson, T. (2007). Prospection: Experiencing the future. *Science, 351,* 1351–1354.

Gilovich, T. (1983). Biased evaluation and persistence in gambling. *Journal of Social and Personal Psychology, 44,* 1110–1126.

Gordin, M., Tilley, H., & Prakash, G. (2010). Utopia and Dystopia beyond space and time. In M. Gordin, H. Tilley, & G. Prakash (Hrsg.), *Conditions of historical possibility.* Princeton University Press.

Graf, H. G. (2003). Was ist eigentlich Zukunftsforschung? *Sozialwissenschaften und Berufspraxis, 26*(4), 355–364.

Gutiérrez, G. (2001). *A theology of liberation.* SCM Press.

Green, J. (2008). *Pragmatism and social hope.* Columbia University Press.

Green, R. (2019). Introduction. In R. Green (Hrsg.), *Theories of hope: Exploring alternative affective dimensions of human experience.* Rowman & Littlefield.

Gruber, P. (2018). *Die Zukunft der Landwirtschaft ist biologisch! Welthunger, Agrarpolitik und Menschenrechte.* Budrich.

Habermas, J. (1985). Die Krise des Wohlfahrtsstaates und die Erschöpfung utopischer Energien. *Die neue Unübersichtlichkeit, Merkur, 39*(431), 141–163.

Halpin, D. (2002). *Hope and education: The role of the utopian imagination.* Routledge.

Hamilton, D. L., & Huffman, L. J. (1971). Generality of impression formation processes for evaluative and nonevaluative judgments. *Journal of Personality and Social Psychology, 20,* 200–207.

Havel, V. (1990). *Briefe an Olga. Betrachtungen aus dem Gefängnis. Reinbeck b.* Rowohlt Taschenbuch

Heinrich, M., Senf, M., & Hüther, G. (2020). *#Education for the Future. Bildung für ein gelingendes Leben.* Goldman.

Herth, K. (1992). Abbreviated instrument to measure hope: Development and psychometric evaluation. *Journal of Advanced Nursing, 17*(10), 1251–1259.

Herth, K. A., & Cutcliffe, J. R. (2002). The concept of hope in nursing 6: Research/education/policy/practice. *British Journal of Nursing, 11*(21), 1404–1411.

Hicks, D. (1994). *Preparing for the future: Notes & queries for concerned educators.* Adamantine Press.

Hicks, D. (1996). Retrieving the dream: How students envision their preferable futures. *Futures, 28*(8), 741–749.

Hicks, D. (2003). *Lessons for the future: The missing dimension in education.* Routledge.

Hinds, P. S., Oakes, L. L., Hicks, J., Powell, B., Srivastava, D. K., Spunt, S. L., Harper, J., Baker, J., West, N., & Furman, W. L. (2009). "Trying to be a good parent" as defined by interviews with parents who made phase I, terminal care, and resuscitation decisions for their children. *Journal of Clinical Oncology, 27*(35), 5979–5985.

Husman, J., & Shell, D. F. (2008). Beliefs and perceptions about the future: A measurement of future time perspective. *Learning and Individual Differences, 18*(2), 166–175.

Hüther, G. (2016). *Biologie der Angst: Wie aus Streß Gefühle werden.* Vandenhoeck & Ruprecht.

James, W. (1979). *The will to believe and other essays in popular philosophy* (Bd. 6). Harvard University Press.

Jungk, R., & Müllert, N. (1989). *Zukunftswerkstätten. Mit Phantasie gegen Routine und Resignation.* Hayne.

Kadlac, A. (2015). The virtue of hope. *Ethical Theory and Moral Practice, 18*(2), 337–354.

Kappes, H. B., & Oettingen, G. (2011). Positive fantasies about idealized futures sap energy. *Journal of Experimental Social Psychology, 47,* 719–729.

Keyes, C. L. (2002). The mental health continuum: From languishing to flourishing in life. *Journal of Health and Social Research, 43,* 207–222.

Kleist, N., & Jansen, S. (2016). Introduction: Hope over time – Crisis, immobility and future-making. *History and Anthropology, 27*(4), 373–392.

Klinger, E., Barta, S. G., & Maxeiner, M. E. (1980). Motivational correlates of thought content frequency and commitment. *Journal of Personality and Social Psychology, 39,* 1222–1237.

Krafft, A. M. (2019). *Werte der Hoffnung: Erkenntnisse aus dem Hoffnungsbarometer.* Springer.

Krafft, A. M., & Walker, A. M. (2018). *Positive Psychologie der Hoffnung: Grundlagen aus Psychologie, Philosophie.* Springer.

Kreibich, R. (2008). *Zukunftsforschung für die gesellschaftliche Praxis* (Arbeitsbericht Nr. 29/2008). Institut für Zukunftsstudien und Technologiebewertung.

Kretz, L. (2019). Hope, the environment and moral imagination. In R. Green (Hrsg.), *Theories of hope: Exploring alternative affective dimensions of human experience* (S. 155–176). Rowman & Littlefield.

Kroenke, K., Spitzer, R. L., Williams, J. B., & Löwe, B. (2009). An ultra-brief screening scale for anxiety and depression: The PHQ-4. *Psychosomatics, 50*(6), 613–621.

Kurzweil, R. (2005). Human life: The next generation. *New Scientist, 24*(9). http://www.singularity.com/NewScienceArticle.pdf.

Lazarus, R. S. (1993). From psychological stress to the emotions: A history of changing outlooks. *Annual Review of Psychology, 44*(1), 1–22.

Lazarus, R. S. (1999). Hope: An emotion and a vital coping resource against despair. *Social Research, 66*(2) 653–678.

Lear, J. (2006). *Radical hope: Ethics in the face of cultural devastation.* Harvard University Press.

Linley, P. A., & Joseph, S. (2011). Meaning in life and posttraumatic growth. *Journal of Loss and Trauma, 16*(2), 150–159.

Marcel, G. (1949). *Homo Viator, Philosophie der Hoffnung.* Bastion.

Markley, O. W., & Harman, W. W. (Hrsg.). (1982). *Changing images of man.* Pergamon Press.

Martin, A. (2019). Interpersonal hope. In C. Blöser & T. Stahl (Hrsg.), *The moral psychology of hope* (S. 229–248). Rowman & Littlefield International.

Masini, E. B. (2000). Futures Research and Sociological Analysis. In S. Quah & A. Sales (Hrsg.), *The International Handbook of Sociology* (S. 491–505). SAGE.

McDonald, J. (2008). The spirit of hope and its near enemy indifference: A phenomenological continuum. In W. Bauman (Hrsg.), *Hope: Global interdisciplinary perspectives.* Papers Presented at the 3rd Global Conference „Hope: Probing the Boundaries", Inter-Disciplinary Press, 39–49.

McGeer, V. (2004). The art of good hope. *The Annals of the American Academy of Political and Social Science, 592*(1), 100–127.

McGeer, V. (2008). Trust, hope and empowerment. *Australasian Journal of Philosophy, 86*(2), 237–254.

McKibben, B. (2007). *Hope, human and wild: True stories of living lightly on the earth.* Milkweed Editions.

Meevissen, Y. M., Peters, M. L., & Alberts, H. J. (2011). Become more optimistic by imagining a best possible self: Effects of a two week intervention. *Journal of Behavior Therapy and Experimental Psychiatry, 42*(3), 371–378.

Meirav, A. (2009). The nature of hope. *Ratio, 22*(2), 216–233.

Miceli, M., & Castelfranchi, C. (2010). Hope: The power of wish and possibility. *Theory & Psychology, 20*(2), 251–276.

Montgomery, G. H., David, D., DiLorenzo, T., & Erblich, J. (2003). Is hoping the same as expecting? Discrimination between hopes and response expectancies for nonvolitional outcomes. *Personality and Individual Differences, 35*(2), 399–409.

Mullen, B., & Johnson, C. (1990). Distinctiveness-based illusory correlations and stereotyping: A meta-analytic integration. *British Journal of Social Psychology, 29,* 11–28.

Nordensvard, J. (2014). Dystopia and disutopia: Hope and hopelessness in German pupils' future narratives. *Journal of Educational Change, 15*(4), 443–465.

Oettingen, G. (1997). *Psychologie des Zukunftsdenkens.* Hogrefe.

Oettingen, G. (2000). Expectancy effects on behavior depend on selfregulatory thought. *Social Cognition, 18,* 101–129.

Oettingen, G. (2012). Future thought and behaviour change. *European Review of Social Psychology, 23,* 1–63.

Oettingen, G. (2014). *Rethinking positive thinking: Inside the new science of motivation.* Penguin Random House.

Oettingen, G., Pak, H., & Schnetter, K. (2001). Self-regulation of goal setting: Turning free fantasies about the future into binding goals. *Journal of Personality and Social Psychology, 80,* 736–753.

Parker-Oliver, D. (2002). Redefining hope for the terminally ill. *American Journal of Hospice and Palliative Medicine, 19*(2), 115–120.

Peters, M. L., Flink, I. K., Boersma, K., & Linton, S. J. (2010). Manipulating optimism: Can imagining a best possible self be used to increase positive future expectancies? *The Journal of Positive Psychology, 5*(3), 204–211.

Pettit, P. (2004). Hope and its place in mind. *The Annals of the American Academy of Political and Social Science, 592*(1), 152–165.

Polak, F. (1973). *The image of the future,* translated from the Dutch and abridged by Elise Boulding. Jossey-Bass/Elsevier.

Reese, B. (2013). *Infinite progress: How the internet and technology will end ignorance, disease, poverty, hunger, and war.* Greenleaf Book Group.

Refle, J.-E. et al. (2020). *First results of the Swiss household panel – Covid-19 study.* FORS Working Paper 2020.

Riner, R. D. (1987). Doing futures research – Anthropologically. *Futures, 19*(3), 311–328.

Rorty, R. (1998). *Achieving our country.* Harvard University Press.

Rorty, R. (1999). *Philosophy and social hope.* Penguin Books.

Rorty, R. (2002). Hope and the future. *Peace Review, 14*(2), 149–155.

Rubin, A. (2002). Reflections upon the late-modern transition as seen in the images of the future held b. young Finns. In J. Gidley, N. Ingwersen, & S. Inayatullah (Hrsg.), *Youth futures: Comparative research and transformative visions* (S. 99–110). Greenwood.

Schumpeter, J. A. (1942). *Kapitalismus, Sozialismus und Demokratie.* UTB (Ausgabe von 2005).

Schwartz, S. H. (2012). An overview of the Schwartz theory of basic values. *Online Readings in Psychology and Culture, 2*(1), 11–20.

Seligman, M. E., Railton, P., Baumeister, R. F., & Sripada, C. (2013). Navigating into the future or driven by the past. *Perspectives in Psychological Science, 8*, 119–141.

Seligman, M. E., Railton, P., Baumeister, R. F., & Sripada, C. (2016). *Homo prospectus.* Oxford University Press.

Shade, P. (2001). *Habits of hope – A pragmatic theory.* Vanderbilt University Press.

Shade, P. (2019). Shame, hope, and the courage to transgress. In R. Green (Hrsg.), *Theories of hope: Exploring alternative affective dimensions of human experience.* Rowman & Littlefield.

Sheldon, K. M., & Lyubomirsky, S. (2006). How to increase and sustain positive emotion: The effects of expressing gratitude and visualizing best possible selves. *Journal of Positive Psychology, 1*(2), 73–82.

Shepperd, J. A., Waters, E. A., Weinstein, N. D., & Klein, W. M. (2015). A primer on unrealistic optimism. *Current Directions in Psychological Science, 24*(3), 232–237.

Siegenthaler, H. (1993). *Regelvertrauen, Prosperität und Krisen: Die Ungleichmäßigkeit wirtschaftlicher und sozialer Entwicklung als Ergebnis individuellen Handelns und sozialen Lernens.* Mohr.

Šimečka, M. (1984). *The Restoration of Order: The Normalization of Czechoslovakia, 1969–1976.* Verso.

Slaughter, R. A. (1993). The substantive knowledge base of futures studies. *Futures – Guildford, 25,* 227.

Slaughter, R. A. (1994). Changing images of futures in the 20th century. In D. Hicks (Hrsg.), *Preparing for the future – Notes & queries for concerned educators* (S. 39–59). Adamantine Press Ltd.

Snow, N. E. (2018). Hope as a democratic civic virtue. *Metaphilosophy, 49*(3), 407–427.

Snow, N. E. (2019). Faces of hope. In R. Green (Hrsg.), *Theories of hope: Exploring alternative affective dimensions of human experience* (S. 5–23). Rowman & Littlefield.

Stahl, T. (2019). Political hope and cooperative community. In C. Blöser & T. Stahl (Hrsg.), *The moral psychology of hope* (S. 265–283). Rowman & Littlefield International.

Stewart, C. (2002). Re-Imagining your neighborhood: A model for futures education. In G. Gidley & I. S. Inayatullah (Hrsg.), *Youth futures: Comparative research and transformative visions* (S. 187–196). Greenwood.

Stitzlein, S. (2019). Pragmatist hope. In C. Blöser & T. Stahl (Hrsg.), *The moral psychology of hope* (S. 93–112). Rowman & Littlefield International.

Tedeschi, R. G., & Calhoun, L. G. (1995). *Trauma and transformation. Growing in the aftermath of suffering.* Sage.

Tedeschi, R. G., & Calhoun, L. G. (1996). The Posttraumatic growth inventory: Measuring the positive legacy of trauma. *Journal of Traumatic Stress, 9*(3), 455–471.

Tedeschi, R. G., & Calhoun, L. G. (2004). Posttraumatic growth: Conceptual foundations and empirical evidence. *Psychological Inquiry, 15*(1), 1–18.

Tennen, H., Affleck, G., & Tennen, R. (2002). Clipped feathers: The theory and measurement of hope. *Psychological Inquiry, 13*(4), 311–317.

Toffler, A. (1970). *Der Zukunftsschock: Strategien für die Welt von morgen.* Goldmann.

Vonk, R. (1996). Negativity and potency effects in impression formation. *European Journal of Social Psychology, 26,* 851–865.

Vonk, R. (1999). Differential evaluations of likeable and dislikeable behaviors enacted towards superiors and subordinates. *European Journal of Social Psychology, 29,* 139–146.

Walker, M. (2006). *Moral repair: Reconstructing moral relations after wrongdoing.* Cambridge University Press.

Webb, D. (2008). Exploring the relationship between hope and utopia: Towards a conceptual framework. *Politics, 28*(3), 197–206.

Webb, D. (2013). Pedagogies of hope. *Studies in Philosophy and Education, 32*(4), 397–414.

Weinstein, N. D. (1980). Unrealistic optimism about future life events. *Journal of Personality and Social Psychology, 39*(5), 806–820.

Weinstein, N. D. (1989). Optimistic biases about personal risks. *Science, 246*(4935), 1232–1234.

West, C. (2009). *Hope on a tightrope: Words and wisdom.* SmileyBooks Hay House.

Ziegler, W. (1991). Envisioning the future. *Futures, 23*(5), 516–527.